Teacher's **1B** Guide

Apple Pie
Delta's Beginning ESL Program

Delta Publishing Delta

Sadae Iwataki, Editor

Jean Owensby
Constance Turner
Greta Kojima

REVISED EDITION

© 1994 by Delta Systems Co., Inc.
Revised Edition 1996

ISBN 0–937354–61–9

Delta Systems Co., Inc.
1400 Miller Parkway
McHenry, IL 60050 U.S.A.

Printed in the USA
10 9 8 7 6 5 4

Apple Pie 1B
Table of Contents

Unit Eleven: Food and Fun

Unit Twelve: What's Going On?

To the Teacher

Thank you for choosing Delta's **Apple Pie** as your ESL textbook. This series brings to you a comprehensive, carefully structured, realistically paced curriculum for the "beginning low" and "beginning high" levels, as defined by California's English as a Second Language Model Standards for Adult Education Program, in four books: student book 1A and 1B for beginning low ESL and student books 2A and 2B for beginning high ESL. It is appropriate for adult and young adult learners in the United States and abroad. Its content and structure were developed over many years of use in the adult ESL programs of the Los Angeles Unified School District.

The following is a brief overview of the lesson structure of **Apple Pie**, and general directions for using the teaching notes in this guide.

Something New: Every lesson begins with this oral introduction of new material through use of visuals to accompany a listening comprehension selection. The target vocabulary and structures are introduced without the textbook through a series of steps: listen only, comprehension check, listen and repeat, listen and respond.

Let's Talk: This is a dialogue that incorporates the new language in the meaningful context of a dialogue set in a real–life situation. Students first master the dialogue orally with the help of a dialogue visual, then practice it with and without the teacher's help, and finally practice it with a partner and /or say it aloud from memory.

Practice, Interaction, Practice Activity: These are sections that expand on the language presented in the previous sections by using it again in mini–dialogues for pair practice, situations for role plays, group activities, and mixers. The practice sections move from more controlled oral work to more open–ended or personalized oral practice.

Reading: Reading passages are related to the lesson topic, using similar structures and vocabulary to present new information. They are followed by discussion questions, which generally end with a reference to students' own thoughts or experiences.

Writing: The writing sections provide review and reinforcement while giving students a chance to practice spelling and punctuation. In books 2A and 2B, some lessons have sections called *More Writing*, which provide prompts for controlled or original writing of sentences and short paragraphs.

After the core lesson, it is important to continue using the new language by including the ***Review*** and ***Activity Pages*** in subsequent class sessions. This way students have many opportunities to internalize new structures and functions and use them in their everyday interactions in English. The *Activity Pages* may include focused listening exercises, "information gap" activities, games, mixers, reading and discussion of true stories, and other tasks that integrate the language skills in a variety of relevant, interesting activities which provide student–student interaction and skill–building opportunities.

After each of the eight units of three related lessons, there is an ***Evaluation***, with Listening Comprehension, Reading, and Writing sections. This regular evaluation is meant to be done individually and then corrected to give students an indication of their progress and teachers an indication of the current needs of the class.

An essential element in the pedagogy of **Apple Pie** is the use of the hand–held visuals available for each book. These contain the illustrations for the *Something New* and *Let's Talk* sections of the lessons, and are used to teach new vocabulary, structures, and functions with aural and visual cues for understanding. On the back of each visual are the phrases, sentences, or dialogue to be presented, so that the new language can be introduced as students listen without looking at the textbook.

The *Let's Talk* and *Reading* sections, focused listening sections of the *Activity Pages*, and Listening Comprehension sections of the *Evaluations* also appear on the **Apple Pie Cassette** available to accompany each book. Instructions are given in this teacher's guide for presenting those sections by using the cassette to provide opportunities for students to develop better listening skills by hearing different voices, by hearing new material before they read it, and by doing listening exercises that require them to glean information to carry out a task.

Guide to symbols used in the teacher's guide:

 The "closed book" symbol is a reminder that this is an oral section of the presentation, during which students are not yet looking at their books.

 This symbol means "now open your books" and indicates that students are about to see in print the items that they have been practicing orally.

 This group symbol indicates that students will be moving around the room in an interaction that requires them to speak to several students, or that they will be participating in a group activity.

 A cassette symbol in the heading means that a section is recorded on the tape, allowing an alternative presentation of the section by having students listen to a dialogue, listen while reading a passage, or listen and pick out specific information in a focused listening exercise.

At the beginning of each lesson in the teacher's guide, you will find Communication Objectives for the lesson, new structures that appear in the lesson, and a list of the visuals and other instructional aids needed for presenting the lesson to your class.

Good luck and success to you all. We hope that the **Apple Pie** program will serve you well, and that your students will find learning English our way to be effective, confidence–building and fun!

What's the Matter?

Communication Objectives:
>   Identify parts of the body
>   Ask and answer questions about ailments
>   Express sympathy

Structures:
>   Simple present of *have*

Visuals:
>   V1   a headache
>   V2   an earache
>   V3   a toothache
>   V4   a backache
>   V5   a stomachache
>   V6   Let's Talk: What's the Matter
>   V7   the human body

Page 2

✔ Review: Meeting New Friends

1. Review the basics of self introductions. Model and practice with the class, then a few individual students.

2. Have students interact with one another, introducing themselves.

3. Review basics of introducing a person to another student. Model and practice with the class, then with a few students in front of class.

4. Have students interact with one another, introducing a friend to another student.

Something New: Ailments

1. Briefly explain lesson objectives: To talk about ailments, body parts and expressing sympathy.

2. Ask class "What's the matter?" Hold up V1 and say "I have a headache."

3. Show V1 and have students repeat "I have a headache."

4. Ask again "What's the matter?" Show V1 and elicit "I have a headache."

5. Repeat above steps with V2–V5.

6. Cue with visuals and model again, having class and individuals repeat.

7. Cue with visuals and have class and individual students identify the ailments.

Page 3 **Let's Talk:** What's the Matter?*

 1. Show the dialogue visual to establish the context of the conversation: Two women are talking on the telephone.

2. Explain that sometimes a response to the ritual greeting, "How are you?" can be other than, "Fine."

3. Model the dialogue. Ask questions to check comprehension.

4. Model the dialogue again, having class repeat each line.

5. Take one role and have class take other role; then change roles.

6. Divide class in half and have each half take a role; then have them switch roles.

7. Have groups, then individuals practice dialogue.

8. Write the dialogue on the board and have class copy it.

9. Have class, groups, pairs read the dialogue, taking one role, then the other.

*Cassette users can have students listen to the dialogue first with books closed.

☛ Practice: "I have a stomachache" and "That's too bad"

 1. Have class open books and read the dialogue and the practice items on page 3 in pairs. Explain use of "That's too bad" in expressing sympathy.

2. Students should practice using all 5 visuals from the lesson.

Page 4 ## Something New: I Have a Sore Arm

1. Use the visual of the human body to point out the various parts of the body: shoulder, arm, elbow, etc. (Note: Using a transparency of this visual facilitates class vision and thus understanding.)

2. Say each body part and have students repeat vocabulary words.

3. Say each body part and have students point to the part on themselves.

4. Ask a volunteer to point to body parts as the class calls out the correct vocabulary words.

5. Direct students to draw a line from the vocabulary word to the part of the body.

6. Ask volunteers to draw lines from the words to the body on the transparency or chalkboard.

 7. Have students do the matching in their books.

8. Have students check their work against the transparency or chalkboard.

 9. Act out each ailment, or point to the appropriate body parts on the transparency and model the sentences for each ailment as students listen.

10. Act out each ailment, model the sentence and have students repeat. Be clear about when to use "sore" or "ache."

11. Act out various ailments and have students say the correct sentence.

Page 5 ### ■ **Interaction:** I Have a Backache

1. Model the procedure for pair practice, using a student as the other person in the dyad.

2. Have students practice in pairs. Monitor student progress, giving help as necessary.

★ **Something Extra:** Expressing Sympathy

1. Teach class to react to somebody's ailment by offering sympathy.

2. Give the two ways to offer sympathy.

3. Have class practice.

☞ **Practice: "I'm sorry to hear that"**

 1. Have student volunteers act out various ailments (sore arm, etc.) then go through the dialogues in the practice.

 2. Have class open books and practice exercise as a class, in groups, and in pairs.

3. Write answers to #3 and #4 on the board for students to check their work.

★ Something Extra: Pronunciation

1. Introduce the sound of /ey/ in ache. Model the sound, then the word ache, then the word headache. Use the word in a sentence: "I have a headache." Repeat with other aches.

2. Have students open books and practice as a class, in groups, in pairs. (Go around the room and monitor pairs, modeling sound as necessary.)

■ Interaction: How Are You?

1. Give the directions for the Interaction, modeling and giving examples.

2. Give students a few minutes to complete the activity. Have a few students report their findings to the class.

🖭 Reading: I Feel Terrible*

1. Use the visual accompanying Reading to establish context and for pre–reading predictions.

2. Read the story to the class as students follow along in their books.

3. Ask comprehension questions and then have students read the story again, by themselves.

4. Initiate discussion by asking whole class and/or individuals the questions.

5. Have students continue the discussion in pairs or groups.

*Cassette users can have students listen to the Reading first with books closed.

✍ Writing

1. Assign class to do Writing activity. Explain that they must write the question or answer.

2. Give time for most of class to complete activity.

3. Check Writing as a class.

☛ Practice Activity: Simon says

1. Have class stand up. Give commands and act out responses.

2. Explain that anyone who responds without the "Simon says" add–on must sit down.

3. You might want to have a prize for the student(s) standing at the end of the game.

Delta's Apple Pie, Teacher's Guide 1B

Lesson 25 Activity Page

General Directions

1. Be sure that students understand the purpose of each listening activity. Many are focused listening activities, which require students to listen and pick out specific information.

2. Pair practice and working in teams are integral aspects of the activity pages. Explanations about how to do these activities are important for their success.

Page 9 **A. Listen to the directions and write the number under the correct picture.***

Go over the directions. Make sure that students understand that they need to listen to the dialogue and write the number that matches the picture. Play the tape or read the script at normal conversational speed. After the first reading, check class for comprehension of directions and then the ability to distinguish the ailments. If necessary, go over the directions again and re–read the script.

Script:
Number 1:

Jack:	Hey, Gus … what's the matter?
Gus:	I have a backache.
Jack:	Ah, a backache. That's rough.

Number 2:

Hank:	Hi there, Sara. What's wrong?
Sara:	I have a sore neck.
Hank:	Oh, a sore neck. That's a shame.

Number 3:

Mike:	Maria! How are you?
Maria:	Not so great. I have a headache.
Mike:	A headache. Yeah. I think it's the smog.

Number 4:

Sam:	Mark, what's going on?
Mark:	Aww, I have a bad stomachache.
Sam:	A stomachache? You should see a doctor.

Number 5:

Henry:	How are you feeling, Lionel?
Lionel:	Just great! I feel fine.
Henry:	That's wonderful.

*Cassette users can have students listen to the script on tape.

B. *Partner 1 read the directions. Partner 2 follow the directions. Then change roles.*
Go over the directions with the class. Model once or twice. Have students go into pairs for the practice, with one reading the directions, the other with book closed, following the directions. Students should then reverse tasks.

Do You Have a Fever?

Communication Objectives:
Describe simple medical complaints
Suggest remedies for simple ailments
Read a Fahrenheit thermometer

New Structures:
Yes/No questions with *have*
Short answers *Yes, I do/No, I don't*

Visuals:

V8	a thermometer
V1	a headache
V9	a sore body
V10	a fever
V11	a cough
V12	a runny nose
V13	a sore throat
V14	Let's Talk: Do You Have a Fever?

Other instructional aids:
cold remedies—bottle of aspirin, cough syrup

Page 10

✔ Review: What's the Matter?

Cue with visuals and review various ailments. Review forms with "ache" and "sore."

Something New: What's Your Temperature?

1. Briefly explain lesson objectives: To make simple medical complaints and read an American thermometer.

2. Show the thermometer visual, and explain what it is. Note that in the U.S. Fahrenheit temperatures are used. (A transparency shown on overhead projector will show the temperatures more clearly, or reproduce the thermometer with the temperatures on the board.)

3. Model and have students repeat "thermometer."
   (Note: You may wish to point out that in the U.S. one's temperature is taken by placing the thermometer under the tongue. Elicit how temperature is taken in other countries.)

4. Explain the terms "normal" and "fever." Show the normal reading on the thermometer and say aloud, "Ninety–eight point six." Show temperatures for a fever, saying them aloud: "a hundred," "a hundred and one," etc.

5. Have students repeat the temperature figures, beginning with 98.6 to 106.

6. Ask "What's your temperature?" Point to degrees on the thermometer and elicit answers: "My temperature is normal. It's 98.6" and "My temperature is 101. I have a fever" and similar responses for other temperatures.

Page 11
☞ Practice: "My temperature's 102"

1. Draw a thermometer on the board with appropriate temperature to practice the question, "Do you have a fever?"

2. Practice "Yes, I do" and "No, I don't," using degrees on the thermometer as cues.

3. Have class open their books and practice the exercise. Be sure they answer using "do" and "don't," not "have" or "haven't."

Page 12
Something New: Symptoms

1. Say "I think I have the flu." Have students repeat.

2. Hold up V1 and say "I have a headache." Have students repeat.

3. Do the same with V9 and V10.

4. Again say "I think I have the flu." Have students repeat the symptoms as you show the visuals.

5. Repeat steps 1–4 for "I think I have a cold," using visuals V11–V13.

📼 Let's Talk: Do You Have a Fever?*

1. Show the dialogue visual to establish the context of the conversation: That the person is sick and is calling the doctor.

2. Model the dialogue as students listen, indicating the speakers by pointing to the visual or other means.

3. Model the dialogue again.

4. Model the dialogue and have class repeat.

5. Take one role and have class take other role; then have them switch roles.

6. Divide class in half and have them take the two roles; then have them switch roles.

7. Have volunteers say the dialogue for the class.

 8. Have class open books and practice the dialogue in pairs.

*Cassette users can have students listen to the dialogue first with books closed.

Page 13 ## ★ Something Extra: Suggesting Remedies

1. Ask, "What medicine do you take for the flu/a cold?"

2. Show bottles of aspirin and cold medicine, or point to the illustrations in the book. Model and have class identify and repeat names. Explain uses of the medications. Have class identify medications for the various symptoms.

■ Interaction: Home Remedies

1. Explain the difference between home remedies and store bought remedies. Give examples, (lemon and honey, etc.).

2. Repeat question, "What medicine do you take for…?"

3. Elicit remedies from students.

 4. Have students work in groups to tell each other about ailments and have other students suggest remedies as shown in example in student text.

5. Ask a few students to report back to class on remedies suggested for various ailments.

Page 14 ## Reading: Calling in Sick*

1. Have class look at visual accompanying Reading. Elicit occupations of the two people in dialogue.

2. Read the conversation to the class as students follow along in their books. Check comprehension orally.

3. Have class do the questions independently. Go over the statements as a class.

4. Have class read the selection as a class, in groups, and in pairs.

*Cassette users can have students listen to the Reading first with books closed.

✍ Writing

1. Have class do Writing independently.

2. Correct activity as a class.

Lesson 26 Activity Pages

Page 15 📼 *A. Listen to the nurse and write the correct temperature.**

1. Make sure that class understands they are to write the correct temperature in each case.

2. Repeat script as necessary.

Script:
1. Your temperature's a hundred and one.

2. You don't have a fever. Your temperature's ninety–eight point six.

3. My temperature is a hundred and two. I have a high fever.

4. His temperature is ninety–nine.

5. What's her temperature? It's ninety–seven.

6. She has a temperature of a hundred. It's a slight fever.

*Cassette users can have students listen to the script on tape.

B. Talk about the picture.

This is used as a general discussion activity, so that students can practice the language they know. Use the questions as a guide.

Page 16 ### C. These people have problems. Write the remedy.

Have students read the remedies and copy them under the appropriate picture.

Page 17 ### D. Tic Tac Toe: "What's the Matter?"

Divide the class into two groups: one X and one O. Make a transparency of the grid from the student book, or draw an empty grid on the chalkboard and number the squares 1–9 so students can identify the ailment they mean by number. Ask, "What's the matter?" for each square. Follow the directions for the game as given in the student book. You may want to have prizes for the winning team.

I Have an Appointment with Dr. Chu

Communication Objectives:
>   Make medical appointments
>   Answer questions about health insurance
>   Interpret health insurance card

New Structures:
>   Contrast of *Is it...?/Yes, it is* and
>   *Do You...?/Yes, I do*

Visuals:
>   V15   a medical appointment card
>   V16   a health insurance card
>   V17   Let's Talk: I Have an Appointment

Other instructional aids:
>   medical or dental appointment cards

Page 18

✔ Review: Parts of the Body

1. Ask a volunteer to draw a human body on the chalkboard.

2. Have other volunteers label body parts.

3. Discuss aches and pains and have class suggest remedies.

Something New: An Appointment Card and a Health Insurance Card

1. Briefly explain lesson objectives: To make medical appointments and talk about health insurance.

2. Reproduce appointment card in book on the board. Elicit from class the use of these cards as reminders to patients of their medical or dental appointments. Have class answer oral questions about the card. Read the card together.

3. Have class open their books and look at the appointment card again. Go over the same material, this time having class read the questions and answer them.

4. Reproduce the health insurance card on the board. Explain its use in health care. Ask oral comprehension questions.

5. Have class turn to the health insurance card in the book. Have class read the words on the card together, then answer the questions as a class.

6. Do the discussion questions.

Page 19 ## Let's Talk: I Have an Appointment*

1. Show the visual to establish the context of the conversation: Sara has a doctor's appointment.

2. Model the dialogue as students listen, indicating the speakers by pointing to the visual or other means.

3. Model the dialogue again.

4. Model the dialogue and have class repeat.

5. Take one role and have class take other role; then change roles.

6. Divide class in half and have them take the two roles; then have them switch roles.

7. Have volunteers say the dialogue for the class.

 8. Have class open books and practice the dialogue in pairs.

*Cassette users can have students listen to the dialogue first with books closed.

Page 20 ## ☛ Practice: "I have a 3:30 appointment"

1. Get some sheets of paper to represent appointment cards. Write the times of appointments large enough so that they can be read by the class.

2. Use these to cue practice exercises 1–4.

3. Get a sheet of paper to represent a health card and use this to cue practice exercises 5 and 6.

📼 **Reading:** Late for an Appointment*

1. Go over the sequence of visuals to establish context and have class make predictions as a pre–reading activity.

2. Read the story to the class as students follow along in their books.

3. Go over predictions class made.

4. Initiate discussion by asking whole class and/or individuals the questions.

5. Have students continue the discussion in pairs or groups.

6. Have class read story as a class, in groups, and individually out loud.

*Cassette users can have students listen to the reading first with books closed.

■ Interaction: Your Next Appointment

1. Explain and model the roleplay activity, using a student volunteer. Use a few different days, dates, and times.

2. Have class, then volunteers, practice some sample dialogues before going into pair practice.

✍ **Writing**

1. Have class do Writing independently.

2. Correct as a class.

Page 23 **A. Write the appointment times.***

Go over the directions and make sure that students understand that they need to write the appointment times they hear. Repeat the whole script if necessary.

Script:

1. Your next appointment is Tuesday, May 12, at 10:45.

2. I have a 10:30 appointment with Dr. Cota.

3. He's late for his 4 o'clock appointment with the dentist.

4. What time is it? I have to hurry for my 9:45 doctor's appointment.

5. I have an 11 o'clock appointment with Dr. Smith.

6. Is your dental appointment at 8:30?

7. Your son's next appointment is Wednesday, June 16, at 2:45. Is that all right?

8. We have an opening for a 1:30 appointment with Dr. Lee.

9. The earliest opening we have is Friday, November 3, at 2 p.m.

*Cassette users can have students listen to the script on the tape.

B. Talk about the appointment cards.

 In pairs, students can ask and answer questions about the appointment cards. Model one or two questions first, including those that require *a* instead of *an*.

C. Write the answer.

Students can write answers to the questions either in class or at home.

Page 24 **D. BINGO!!**

This Bingo game is a walking interaction, in which students are expected to go around the class to find someone who can answer yes to each question. When a person gets a row all filled in, he/she shouts BINGO! Model one or two questions as an example.

Unit Nine **Evaluation**

Page 25 *I. Listening Comprehension**

    1. Go over the directions for Part I with students.

    2. Read each item of the script two times, at normal conversational speed.

> **Script:**
> 1. I have a backache.
>
> 2. I have a sore shoulder.
>
> 3. Do you have a sore ankle?
>
> 4. My temperature is a hundred and one.
>
> 5. Do you have a fever?
>
> 6. My next appointment is on Thursday.
>
> 7. I have a 10:30 appointment with Dr. Grey.
>
> 8. Drink a lot of liquids.
>
> *Cassette users can have students listen to the script on the tape.

Page 26 *II. Reading and III. Writing*

    1. Go over the directions for Parts II and III with students.

    2. Have class do these sections independently.

Evaluation Check

    1. Correct evaluation by having student volunteers write their answers on the board or an overhead transparency.

    2. Have class check their answers.

    3. Circulate to make sure students have checked their work accurately.

Ana's Our First Child

Communication Objectives:
Talk about one's family
Talk about others' families

New Structures:
Questions with *have*
Short answers with *does/doesn't*

Visuals:
V18   The Vega Family Tree
V19   Let's Talk: Ana's Our First Child

Page 28

✔ Review: Calling in Sick

1. Use visuals V1–V5 from Lesson 25 to review ailments.

2. Explain the importance of letting employers know when an employee can't work because of illness.

3. Model sample dialogue for letting supervisor at work know of absence.

4. Have pair practice, with partners taking turns being supervisor and the person calling in sick.

Something New: Family Tree

1. Establish the objective of the lesson: Students will talk about families.

2. On the board, draw the Vega family tree and explain what a family tree is.

3. Introduce Manuel and Jenny Vega, and introduce their children: Mario, Tony, and Elsa.

4. Have class identify the people as you ask questions about the relationships in the family: Who are the children of Manuel and Jenny Vega? Sons? Daughter?

5. Discuss marital relationships: Who is married and who is single.

6. Have class open their books to see the family tree. Go over the relationships again, having students point to the various persons who are being described: e.g., "Point to Manuel and Jenny's Daughter."

7. Review all the family vocabulary and have students repeat.

Page 29 ☛ **Practice Activity: The Vega family**

1. Go over the directions with students to make sure they understand what to do.

 2. Break the class into groups. Check to see that each group is on task.

3. Ask a volunteer in each group to answer one of the questions for the whole class.

🔲 Let's Talk: Ana's Our First Child*

 1. Show the visual to establish the context of the conversation: Mario Vega is showing pictures of his baby.

2. Model the dialogue as students listen, indicating the speakers by pointing to the visual or other means.

3. Model the dialogue again.

4. Model the dialogue and have class repeat.

5. Take one role and have class take other role; then change roles.

6. Divide class in half and have them take the two roles; then have them switch roles.

7. Have volunteers say the dialogue for the class.

 8. Have class open books and practice the dialogue in pairs.

*Cassette users can have students listen to the dialogue first with books closed.

Page 30 ☛ **Practice: "Do you have any children?"**

 1. Sketch stick figures or rough drawings of the various situations represented by the practice and use these to cue practices. Include both "Do" and "Does" questions.

 2. Practice orally as a whole class, in groups, and pairs; then have class open their books and read what they have been practicing orally, as a class, in groups, and in pairs.

3. Explain the use of "any" in #6 to show a negative. The word "children" need not be repeated after "any."

■ Interaction: Do You Have a Large Family?

1. Model questions and have class practice sample questions. Select one or two students to answer questions. Have class ask you a few of the questions.

 2. Monitor groups as they practice. After the class gets together again, have a few students report their findings.

★ Something Extra: Relationships

1. Have class look at the Vega family tree on page 28 again. Review relationships of uncle, aunt, niece, nephew, and cousins. Give class opportunity for practice: Asking and answering questions about the family members.

2. Have class look at Manuel and Jenny Vega and Ana, Roberto, and Rita, introducing the terms grandparents (grandmother and grandfather) and grandchildren (granddaughter, grandson) and have students repeat. Provide practice.

3. Introduce the various terms for in–laws (father–in–law, sister–in–law, etc.), relating terms to the people in the family and have students repeat. Provide practice.

4. Have class open their books to page 31 to read about the relationships they have been practicing orally.

☛ Practice Activity: Relationships

1. Make sure students understand directions.

2. Have students work independently and then check their answers with partners, in a group or as a class.

📼 Reading: The Single Parent*

1. Have class read the title and ask if they can define it. Read the selection and have students follow along in their books.

2. Ask oral comprehension questions.

3. Have students read the selection on their own.

*Cassette users can have students listen to the reading first with books closed.

Discussion

1. Go over questions with the class.

2. Lead a discussion about single parenthood.

✍ Writing

1. Go over directions with students.

2. Have class do Writing independently, helping individual students as needed.

3. Correct activity in class.

Page 33   ## ☛ Practice Activity: Who's this?

1. Explain how to draw a family tree, using yourself as a model.

2. Have class do the activity.

3. Have students work in pairs and talk about their family trees to their partners.

Page 34 **A. Listen and write the missing names on Milly's family tree.***

1. Have students look at family tree and identify Milly. Check to see that class understands where siblings, parents and children go on the tree.

2. Read the script: Check after reading the name Bob to see that students know where to write the missing name. You will probably need to read the script two or three times.

   Script:
   This is Milly's family tree. Find Milly on the tree. Her husband's name is Bob. Write in his name – Bob.

   Milly and Bob have two children, a son and a daughter. Her son is Charles and her daughter is Sara. Write in her daughter's name – Sara.

   Milly's father is Joe. Her mother is Hannah. Write in her mother's name – Hannah.

   Milly has one sister. Her name is Ruth. Ruth is married. Her husband's name is Karl. Write in Ruth's husband's name – Karl.

   Ruth and Karl have a son. His name is Gary. Write in Ruth and Karl's son's name – Gary.

   Milly's mother–in–law is Martha and her father–in–law is Frank. Write in her father–in–law's name – Frank.

   Bob has a sister. She is Milly's sister–in–law. Her name is Sue. Write in Milly's sister–in–law's name – Sue. Sue is single. She doesn't have any children.

3. Go over the family tree with the names filled in and ask questions about the family.

   *Cassette users can have students listen to the script on the tape.

Page 35 **B. Write questions or answers about Milly's family.**

Have class do writing independently.

Lesson 29

How Many Bedrooms Are There in Your Apartment?

Communication Objectives:
> Identify rooms of a house
> Describe a house or apartment
> Talk about housing desired

New Structures:
> *There is/there are*
> Simple present of *want*

Visuals:

V20	a living room
V21	a dining room
V22	a bedroom
V23	a kitchen
V24	a bathroom
V25	a closet
V26	floor plan
V27	Let's Talk: How Many Bedrooms Are There?

Page 36

✔ Review: A Family Tree

1. Draw your family tree on an overhead transparency or on the chalkboard.

2. Tell the class about your family and have volunteers fill in the names of your relatives.

3. Model how students can ask you about your relatives. Encourage them to ask you questions about your family.

Something New: Rooms in an Apartment

1. Briefly explain the objectives of the lesson: To describe a house or apartment.

2. Show V20 and say "It's a living room." Repeat "living room" and have students repeat.

3. Show V21 and say "It's a dining room." Repeat "dining room" and have students repeat.

4. Do the same for V22–V25.

5. Review all 6 visuals by asking "What is it?"

Page 37 ☛ **Practice: "It's a living room"**

1. Show the first visual and ask questions to elicit vocabulary.

2. Have volunteers form questions about the picture for class to answer.

 3. Have students open books and read individually and/or in pairs what has been practiced orally.

4. Students can practice using all 6 visuals from the lesson.

Something New: Mario and Carol's Apartment

 1. Briefly explain lesson objective: That students will be able to describe a house or apartment. Explain "floor plan."

2. Cue with visual, on a transparency, or on the blackboard. Point to each area of the apartment. Elicit a response. Have students repeat correct responses.

Page 38 ☛ **Practice: "Is there a kitchen in the apartment?"**

1. Cue with the floor plan and follow usual Practice procedure to ask the questions in the Practice, having class practice asking and answering the questions.

 2. Have class open their books to read what they have been practicing orally in the first two pages of the lesson. You may need to discriminate between "Is it?" and Is there?" and "Are they?" and Are there?"

🎞 Let's Talk: How Many Bedrooms Are There?*

 1. Show the visual to establish the context of the conversation: Mario is talking to a friend at work.

2. Model the dialogue as students listen, indicating the speakers by pointing to the visual or other means. Explain *vacancy*.

3. Model the dialogue again.

4. Model the dialogue and have class repeat.

5. Take one role and have class take other role; then change roles.

6. Divide class in half and have them take the two roles; then have them switch roles.

7. Have volunteers say the dialogue for the class.

 8. Have class open books and practice the dialogue in pairs.

*Cassette users can have students listen to the dialogue first with books closed.

Page 39 ☞ **Practice: "Is your apartment small?"**

1. After the dialogue, continue the question and answer drill with a few students. Again, discriminate between "Yes, it is" and "Yes, there is" and "Yes, they are" and "Yes, there are."

2. Have students continue the question and answer pattern, or have them open their books and practice with a partner.

■ **Interaction:** A Floor Plan

1. Draw a floor plan of your home on the chalkboard. Describe the floor plan as you draw.

2. Instruct students to draw a floor plan of their partner's house or apartment.

3. Model how students will ask and answer questions about their homes.

4. If possible, make an overhead transparency of student drawings and have them explain each other's residences. Otherwise, students can reproduce their drawings on the board, or work in groups to describe their drawings.

Page 40 **Reading:** An Apartment or a House*

1. Have class look at visuals accompanying reading selection.

2. Take a poll of class to determine which is Nina's present home.

3. Have class read story as a group or independently.

4. Ask oral comprehension questions.

*Cassette users can have students listen to the Reading first with books closed.

Discussion

1. Go over questions with class.

2. Lead discussion.

✍ **Writing:** My Dream Home

 1. Explain the term "dream" house/home.

 2. Have class draw a floor plan of this ideal and share this plan with a partner.

 3. Have a volunteer or two draw plan on board and tell the class about it. Ask questions about the plan, or have student volunteers ask questions for the class or individual students to answer.

Lesson 29 Activity Pages

  A. Listen and label the picture. Write the names of the rooms on the floor plan.*

 1. Go over the floor plan with the class and explain that they are to listen and write in the names of the missing rooms. Explain that the apartment manager is showing the rooms and describing the apartment.

 2. Read script two times, then as a class fill in the missing rooms. Have a volunteer describe the apartment.

> **Script:**
> Yes, we have a large apartment for rent. Come into the apartment.
>
> Look at the large living room.
>
> Now let's go into the kitchen. This apartment has a dining room. It's next to the kitchen.
>
> Let's go into the hall.
>
> There are three bedrooms and two bathrooms in this apartment.
>
> The large bedroom is the master bedroom. It has its own bathroom and large closet.
>
> There are two bedrooms across the hall. Each of the bedrooms has a closet. There's a bathroom between the two bedrooms.
>
> It's a very nice apartment.

*Cassette users can have students listen to the script on the tape.

Page 43   **B. Read and circle the correct word. Copy the correct sentence.**

        1. Go over the directions with students.

        2. Have students do the writing independently and check as a class.

Page 44 & 45   **C. Information Gap: How many bedrooms are there?**

        1. Direct students to work in pairs.

        2. One student looks at page 44 and covers page 45 and vice–versa.

        3. Have pairs take turns asking questions about the missing information in their grids, then fill in the grid with the information their partners give them.

Is There a Bus Stop Nearby?

Communication Objectives:
> Ask about a rental unit
> Interpret abbreviations in rental ads

New Structures:
> Adverb *nearby*

Visuals:
> V28   a furnished apartment
> V29   an unfurnished apartment
> V30   Let's Talk: Is There a Bus Stop Nearby?

Page 46

✔ Review: A Floor Plan

1. Have a student volunteer draw a diagram of his/her residence and describe it to the class.

2. Have other students ask and answer questions about the home.

Something New: New Apartment

1. State the objectives of the lesson: Students will talk about rentals and read ads.

2. Establish the context for the lesson by talking about getting an apartment or house. Ask and elicit responses for questions:
> T: Do you need a new apartment?
> What kind of apartment do you want?

3. Hold up V28 and say "I want a furnished apartment." Repeat "a furnished apartment" and have students repeat.

4. Hold up V29 and say "I want an unfurnished apartment." Repeat "an unfurnished apartment" and have students repeat.

5. Briefly explain prefix "un" means "not" and give examples (unhappy, unmarried, etc.).

6. Ask and elicit responses:
> T: How do you find a new apartment? (ask friends, see signs on apartment buildings)

7. Introduce the signs in text by reproducing them on chalkboard. Discuss each sign, where it could be seen. Explain the meanings of words. Go over each line and have class read what the sign says.

8. Go over the abbreviations, the ones in the signs and the other ones in the text – Apt., Ba.

9. You may want to give a little quiz, having class write the abbreviation as you dictate the word. Use visuals with the words, if possible.

 10. Have class open books and read what they have been practicing orally.

Page 48 **Let's Talk:** Is There a Bus Stop Nearby?*

1. Show the visual to establish the context of the conversation: Mario and Carol are talking to an apartment manager.

2. Model the dialogue as students listen, indicating the speakers by pointing to the visual or other means.

3. Model the dialogue again. Explain "nearby." Explain why there is no "s" on <u>bedroom</u>. (It's used as an adjective here.)

4. Model the dialogue and have class repeat.

5. Take one role and have class take other role; then change roles.

6. Divide class in half and have them take the two roles; then have them switch roles.

7. Have volunteers say the dialogue for the class.

 8. Have class open books and practice the dialogue in pairs.

*Cassette users can have students listen to the dialogue first with books closed.

Page 48 & 49 ☛ **Practice: "I want a two–bedroom apartment"** and **"How much is the rent?"**

1. Reproduce the signs to use as cues for practice.

2. Practice as class, in groups, and as individuals.

☛ **Practice: "Is there a school nearby?"**

 1. Use visuals to cue practice. Practice as class, in groups, individually.

 2. Have class open their books and read Practice exercises in usual way.

3. If you have visuals of other community places, use them for extra practice.

☛ **Practice Activity: Apartment for rent**

1. Guide the students by asking the class the questions and checking their answers.

2. Review rental abbreviations.

3. Instruct students to make a for rent sign for their house or apartment.

4. Have students write their signs on the board.

Page 50 ■ **Interaction:** Calling the Manager

1. Have class look at the Apts. for Rent sign in book. Establish with class where such a sign would appear, what number to call for information.

2. As a class, discuss what kind of information one would want to get: Number of bedrooms and bathrooms, amenities that are nearby (bus, school, market, etc.), rent, etc. You might list these on the chalkboard as cues.

3. Have class formulate questions that would elicit desired information: Do you have a 2–bedroom apartment? etc.

4. Have volunteer call you (the manager) to ask the questions while you answer them.

5. Have class practice in pairs, taking turns in the roles of prospective tenant and landlord.

🔲 **Reading:** A Three–story Building*

1. Have class look at visual of the apartment building. Have them count the number of floors. [Note: Point out that in the U.S. the ground floor is usually the first floor.] Explain that a story is a floor.

2. Read the story to the class as students follow along in their books. Ask comprehension questions about the reading. Ask yes–no, either–or, and Wh– questions. Go over the Discussion questions as a class.

3. You may want to have a volunteer or two tell the story without reading it.

4. Have class read the story, as a class, in groups, and individually.

*Cassette users can have students listen to the Reading first with books closed.

Page 51   ✍ **Writing**

Have class do Writing exercise A. independently. Circulate and help those who need it. Assign those who finish A. to go ahead with exercise B. Correct the exercises as a class.

Lesson 30 Activity Page

Page 52 🖭 **A. Listen and check the information you hear.***

Direct students to fill in the information they will hear about each person. Read about first person. Go over the information as a class; then read the script. Read script two times. Then go over information.

Script:
1. My name's Ky Luong. I'm single and I want a 1–bedroom 1–bath apartment near my school.

2. My name's Carlos Santana. I'm married and I want a large apartment, a 3–bedroom 2–bath apartment. We have 4 children, so we want to be near a school.

3. My name's Magda Walenska. I'm a grandmother and I have 6 children and 10 grandchildren. I have a small apartment but I want a large house with 3 bedrooms and 2 bathrooms. I don't drive. I need to be near a bus stop.

4. My name's Felix. I'm divorced. I want a 2–bedroom apartment so that I can have a roommate. I need 2 bathrooms, one bathroom for me and one for my roommate. I don't want to be near a mall or a school.

*Cassette users can have students listen to the script on the tape.

B. Match the people with the homes they want. Look at the chart above and write the correct name under the sign.

1. Students will match the people in Exercise A to the ads in Exercise B.

Unit Ten Evaluation

Page 53 **I. Listening Comprehension***

      1. Go over the directions for Part I with students.

      2. Read each item of the script two times, at normal conversational speed.

          Script:
          1. We have a small family.

          2. I want a house.

          3. Carol is Tony's wife.

          4. Elsa is Tony's sister.
            [Note: This is only clear if students can look back at page 28.]

          5. It's a furnished apartment.

          6. Is there a school nearby?

          7. Are there two bathrooms in this house?

          8. Does she have any children?

      *Cassette users can have students listen to the script on the tape.

Page 54 **II. Reading and III. Writing**

      1. Go over the directions for Part II and III with students.

      2. Have class do these sections independently.

Evaluation Check

      1. Correct evaluation by having student volunteers write their answers on the board or an overhead transparency.

      2. Have class check their answers.

      3. Circulate to make sure students have checked their work accurately.

Lesson 31

We Love Mandy's Southern Fried Chicken

Communication Objectives:
Identify preferences for ordering chicken
Place and take orders

New Structures:
Questions with *like* and *want*

Visuals:
V31   a chicken
V32   drumstick and thigh
V33   wing and breast
V34   Let's Talk: At Mandy's

Page 56   ✔ **Review:** Your Home

1. Explain to class that students are going to ask and answer questions about their homes.

2. Go over questions to make sure students understand vocabulary.

3. Have students ask each other questions in groups.

4. Have a representative from each group tell the class about homes in the group.

Page 57   **Something New:** Parts of a Chicken

1. Explain lesson objective: Students will identify preferences for ordering chicken, place and take orders.

2. Show visual of whole chicken. Ask class where they see chicken for sale, eliciting that they can see and buy chicken at a market, or they can buy chicken at places like Kentucky Fried Chicken™, Pollo Loco™, etc.

3. Use visual of whole chicken. Identify the various parts: wing, breast, drumstick, thigh, back. Have students repeat. If it doesn't make you uncomfortable, you can delineate these parts on your body.

4. Use the visuals of the pieces of fried chicken, along with the whole chicken, and model the names of each piece. Show which pieces are dark meat, which are white meat.

5. Have students identify the parts of the chicken as you call out the names, by pointing to the appropriate visuals. Do the same for the white meat/dark meat categories.

6. Ask yes–no and either–or questions about the chicken pieces.

7. Model and have class, groups, individuals repeat.

8. Ask and have class, groups, individuals answer to identify pieces.

Page 58 ☛ **Practice: "I like white meat"**

1. Talk about yourself/your family and your preferences about chicken.

> T: I like chicken. I like white meat.
>   My mother/etc. likes chicken, too.
>   She likes dark meat. etc.

2. Have individual students talk about their preferences.

> S1: I like chicken. I like dark meat.
> C1: S1 likes chicken. He likes dark meat.
> S2: etc.

3. Have class practice questions: Do you…/ Does…? and responses: Yes, I do/he does, etc.

4. Tell what your favorite part of a chicken is; ask several students what theirs is.

5. Have students open their books and go over the words with the visuals. Go over the Practice, as a class, in groups, and in pairs. Explain "both" in #3.

Page 59 **Let's Talk:** At Mandy's *

1. Show the visual to establish the context of the conversation: Mrs. Kim is ordering take–out chicken.

2. Model the dialogue as students listen, indicating the speakers by pointing to the visual or other means.

3. Model the dialogue again.

4. Model the dialogue and have class repeat.

5. Take one role and have class take other role; then change roles.

6. Divide class in half and have them take the two roles; then have them switch roles.

7. Have volunteers say the dialogue for the class.

 8. Have class open books and practice the dialogue in pairs.

*Cassette users can have students listen to the dialogue first with books closed.

Page 60 ☛ **Practice: "I'd like three pieces"**

 1. On paper in print large enough to be read by class as cues, write up various orders (3–piece meal, two pieces of white meat, etc.)

 2. Cue with visuals to practice as a class, in groups, in pairs. Have class open their books to practice exercises. Explain "I'd like" is the same as "I want."

3. Use the menu written on chalkboard or up on screen and have students roleplay clerk and customer. Have class practice together first, then have students practice in pairs.

Page 61 ■ **Interaction:** Taking an Order

1. Establish the context for the Interaction: Ordering and taking an order in a fast food restaurant.

2. Model.

3. Direct students to menu on page 59.

4. Have them work in pairs, giving and taking orders.

☛ **Practice Activity: Planning a party**

1. Go over the questions with the class. Go over the grid.

 2. Have students work in groups.

3. Have groups tell about their parties.

Page 62 🔊 **Reading:** Chicken Is Healthy*

1. Use the visual to establish context and for pre–reading predictions.

2. Have class read story by themselves.

3. Ask comprehension questions and then have students read the story again.

*Cassette users can have students listen to the Reading first with books closed.

Discussion

1. Go over questions.

2. Lead class discussion.

✍ Writing

1. Have students do Writing independently, helping individuals as needed.

2. Go over Writing by having volunteers write questions and answers on board.

Lesson 31 Activity Page

Page 63 🎞 **A. Listen and make a check under the order for each family.***

Explain to class that they are listening to customers' orders. Read each item two times.

Script:
1. I'd like 12 pieces of chicken and an order of potatoes.

2. I'd like 8 pieces of chicken and an order of coleslaw.

3. Please give me 15 pieces of chicken. We don't want mashed potatoes, but we want coleslaw. Oh, and I'd like 1 lunch special also.

4. Can I get a bucket of chicken and a pint of coleslaw? Oh, and some mashed potatoes, too.

5. Let's see. Do I want the barrel ... no, the bucket ... no ... Okay. Give me a box of chicken and a lunch special ... Oh, and throw in an order of mashed potatoes.

*Cassette users can have students listen to the script on the tape.

B. Ask and answer the questions with your partner. Circle the answers.
Model activity before students go into pairs.

He Likes Italian Food

Communication Objectives:
> Express likes and dislikes in food
> Talk about international foods

New Structures:
> Adjectives *hungry* and *thirsty*
> Adjectives *Mexican*, *Japanese*, etc.

Visuals:
> V35   Italian food (pizza and spaghetti)
> V36   Chinese food (chow mein and lemon chicken)
> V37   Japanese food (sushi and teriyaki chicken)
> V38   Mexican food (tostada and taco)
> V39   American food (fried chicken and a hamburger)
> V40   Armenian food (shishkebab and pita bread)
> V41   Let's Talk: What Do You Want to Eat?

Page 64
✔ Review: Pieces of Chicken

1. Use visuals from Lesson 31 as cues to review names of pieces of chicken.

2. Have class open their books and complete the review exercise. See that they understand that some use the singular pronoun, some the plural.

3. Correct the exercise.

Page 65
Something New: International Foods

1. Explain the objectives of the lesson: Students will be able to express likes and dislikes in food and talk about international food.

2. Show each visual, explain what each food item is, and say the foods nationality. Have students repeat.

3. Point to the food, then have students answer yes or no to identify the various visuals.

> T: Point to the Chinese food.
>   Is this Armenian food?

4. Ask either–or questions: Is this Mexican food or Italian food?

5. Have students repeat as you model the various nationalities of foods.

6. Ask wh– questions and have class, groups, individuals identify the various nationalities of foods.

7. Ask yes/no questions, such as "Do you like Italian food?"

☛ Practice: "Mary likes American food"

1. Use visuals V35–V40 to cue practice. Cover half of ethnic food visual to contrast "like" for the general (ethnic food) and "want" for the specific (today). Practice with pronouns I, We, He, She, They.

2. Practice as a class, groups, individuals.

3. Ask various students about ethnic food(s) they like, what they want to eat today. Use the students' responses to cue practice on third person singular statements.

 4. Have class open their books and read what they have been practicing orally.

Page 66 ### *Discussion*

1. Go over questions.

2. Lead class discussion.

📼 Let's Talk: What Do You Want to Eat?*

1. Show the visual to establish the context of the conversation: Tom and Sam are ready for lunch.

2. Model the dialogue as students listen, indicating the speakers by pointing to the visual or other means. Explain "favorite."

3. Model the dialogue again.

4. Model the dialogue and have class repeat.

5. Take one role and have class take other role; then change roles.

6. Divide class in half and have them take the two roles; then have them switch roles.

7. Have volunteers say the dialogue for the class.

8. Have class open books and practice the dialogue in pairs.

*Cassette users can have students listen to the dialogue first with books closed.

Page 67 ☛ **Practice: "Are you hungry?"**

 1. Use visuals to cue practice. Contrast the responses to "Are/Is" and "Do/Does" questions. You may want to teach this difference by writing the first part of each type of question on the board with the appropriate response.

2. Give class opportunity to formulate questions as well as responses.

 3. Have class open their books to read what they have been practicing orally and practice in usual manner. Note negative response in #3. Give other such examples.

★ Something Extra: I'm Thirsty

1. Have students look at the illustrations in the book and practice the pronunciation of *thirsty*. Lead a whole class practice of
"I'm thirsty. I want _____."
"He/she is thirsty. He/she wants _____."

2. If you feel you would like the class to have extra practice with the "be" verb contrasted with "Do/Does," practice questions with the statements as well.

3. Go over discussion questions. Ask students about drinks they like (general) and want (now or at the break), and use their responses for further practice of the target structures.

4. Have class read what they have been practicing orally.

Page 68 **Reading:** International Foods*

1. Introduce in usual way: Pre–reading discussion, independent reading, and follow–up discussion. Ask oral comprehension questions.

2. Have class, individuals read aloud, if you feel it is important to do so.

*Cassette users can have students listen to the Reading first with books closed.

Discussion

1. Go over questions with class.

2. Lead class discussion.

✍ Writing

1. Have class do Writing independently.

2. Correct exercise as a class.

Page 69 ## ✍✍ More Writing

Encourage students who finish the Writing exercise early to do this activity. As they finish, you may want to read their writing and make comments, correcting grammar, spelling, and punctuation as appropriate.

Lesson 32 Activity Pages

Page 70 ### A. Listen to Mark talk about his friends.*
Go over directions with the class. Do the first one as an example.

Script:
My friends Lola, Kumiko, Carla, and Ben like different foods.

Lola likes Italian food, but she doesn't like Japanese food. She likes American food, but she really likes Italian food.

Kumiko is from Japan, so of course she likes Japanese food, but she likes Italian and American food, too.

Carla doesn't like Italian food or Japanese food. She doesn't like American food either. She doesn't like to eat!

Ben likes pizza and sushi, but he doesn't like hamburgers or hot dogs. I guess he likes Italian and Japanese food, but he doesn't like American food.

*Cassette users can have students listen to the script on the tape.

B. Look at the grid and answer the questions.
1. Go over the listening activity above so that students can answer the questions.

2. Volunteers can read their answers to the class or write them on the board.

Page 71 ### C. Guess! What kind of food is it?
Have students form groups of three. Each student should write his/her guesses, compare with the group and correct.
Answers: 1. c, 2. f, 3. e, 4. a, 5. g, 6. d, 7. b

D. Group Grid

 Go over directions to see that students know what to do in groups.

Page 72 ### E. Plan a party.

1. Students also work in groups for this activity.

 2. Direct them to discuss their plans, using the list under "E."

3. Students each then fill out their own invitation forms.

4. You might want to have a volunteer from each group read their invitation to the class or draw it on the board for everyone to see. This is a particularly nice activity if someone in class is artistic.

Page 73 ### F. Write a story about your party.

Students can do this activity individually or in groups.

G. Draw a picture of your party. Show it to your partner and talk about it.

Students might be reluctant at first, but most usually enjoy drawing and especially describing what is going on at their parties.

Lesson 33

I Like American Movies

Communication Objectives:
   Talk about likes and dislikes in movies
   Make suggestions about entertainment

New Structures:
   Let's to suggest or invite

Visuals:

V42	I like action movies.
V43	Sue and Micki like cartoons.
V44	Jim is crazy about westerns.
V45	Henry likes horror movies.
V46	My wife and I love science fiction movies.
V47	My mother loves comedies.
V48	Let's Talk: Let's Rent a Movie

Other instructional aids:
   video cassettes

Page 74

✔ Review: Food from Different Countries

1. Use visuals from Lesson 32 to review ethnic designations for foods.

2. Refer to the various nationalities in class to talk about food from those countries.

3. Have students meet in small groups to talk about foods from their respective countries.

4. Have volunteers report on each group's foods. You or a student can list the foods on the board.

Something New: Kinds of Movies

1. Briefly state objectives of the lesson: Students will talk about likes and dislikes in movies.

2. Show each visual, showing the title of the film. Model the name for the type of movie. Have students repeat the type of movie each time.
   1. action movies   2. cartoons   3. westerns
   4. horror movies   5. science fiction movies   6. comedies

3. Ask who in the class likes each type of film; give visuals to these students and have them repeat the sentences as you prompt them:

  T (to S1): I like action movies.
    S1: I like action movies.

  T (to C1): I like action movies.
    C1: I like action movies.

  T (to C1): S1 likes action movies.
    C1: S1 likes action movies.

    T: S2 and S3 like cartoons. etc.

Page 75 📼 **Let's Talk:** Let's Rent a Movie*

1. Show the dialogue visual to establish the idea of renting a movie at a video store.

2. Draw the faces on the board for Mila and Hank. Model the dialogue as students listen indicating the speakers by pointing to the drawing.

3. Model the dialogue again. Explain "crazy about" something. Explain the use of "Let's" for a suggestion.

4. Model the dialogue and have class repeat.

5. Take one role and have class take other role; then change roles.

6. Divide class in half and have them take the two roles; then have them switch roles.

7. Have volunteers say the dialogue for the class.

8. Have class open books and practice the dialogue in pairs.

*Cassette users can have students listen to the dialogue first with books closed.

☛ Practice: "Do you like horror movies?"

1. Use movie visuals to cue practice. Practice Do/Does questions with "like."

2. Practice the grammatical structure "Let's" to make suggestions, using the video visual.

■ Interaction: Movies

1. Give instructions for the Interaction by drawing grid on chalkboard and practicing questions: Do you like movies? What kind of movies do you like? Fill in grid with information after you and volunteers ask one or two students the questions.

2. Have individuals ask each other the questions and have volunteers report what they found out about some of the others in class.

★ Something Extra: Making Suggestions

1. Review that we use the term "Let's" to make suggestions, and respond to suggestions. Ask class to think about videos and what they would like to do. Elicit ideas:

   > e.g.,   Let's rent a movie.
   >   Let's rent a horror movie.

   While watching the movie:

   > Let's turn up/down the sound.
   > Let's turn off the light. etc.

2. Give examples of appropriate responses.

3. Have students practice in pairs, making and responding to suggestions.

4. Have volunteers read their suggestions to the class. You or a student can write the suggestions and responses on the board so that students can get various ideas and check their work.

▣ Reading: A Movie Rating Guide for Parents*

1. This is a difficult reading selection. Students may need to be guided into understanding it. If class has difficulty in understanding, explain each type of rating using a grid to clarify meaning. Ask comprehension questions: yes–no, either–or, and wh–.

Abbreviation	Type of Rating	Meaning of Rating
G	General	For the whole family
PG	Parental Guidance	Parents can decide
Etc.		

*Cassette users can have students listen to the Reading first with books closed.

Discussion

1. Go over questions.

2. Discuss whether students use ratings in selecting movies and whether they think the rating system is a good idea.

Page 78
■ Interaction: Movie Ratings

 1. Have class look at visuals at the beginning of the lesson. Working in groups, have students discuss visuals using questions on page 78.

2. Have groups report to class.

✍ Writing

1. Explain that students will write about movies and foods they and a fellow classmate like and don't like.

2. Write statements on the board as examples.

Lesson 33 Activity Pages

Page 79
A. Tell the story to your partner.
Elicit the story derived from the illustrations as a class, first orally, and then write it on the board.

Page 80
B. Match the statements to the people in the pictures on page 79.
Refer to the story to fill in the correct answers.

Unit Eleven **Evaluation**

Page 81 *I. Listening Comprehension**

    1. Go over the directions for Part I with students.

    2. Read each item of the script two times, at normal conversational speed.

Script:

    1. I'd like two pieces of white meat.

    2. He likes Italian food.

    3. I'm hungry.

    4. She loves action movies.

    5. Do you want a hamburger?

    6. Is Ana thirsty?

    7. What does he want to eat?

    8. What does Tom like?

*Cassette users can have students listen to the script on the tape.

Page 82 *II. Reading and III. Writing*

    1. Go over the directions for Parts II and III with students.

    2. Have class do these sections independently.

Evaluation Check

    1. Correct evaluation by having student volunteers write their answers on the board or an overhead transparency.

    2. Have class check their answers.

    3. Circulate to make sure students have checked their work accurately.

Lesson 34

You Need a Heavy Jacket

Communication Objectives:
Identify items of clothing
Describe items of clothing
Identify seasons of the year and clothing needed

New Structures:
Simple present of *need*
Adjectives *short/long*, *new/old*, etc.

Visuals:
V49   a short dress
V50   a long skirt
V51   a new suit
V52   an old shirt
V53   a narrow tie
V54   a wide belt
V55   a light coat
V56   a heavy jacket
V57   Let's Talk: You Need a Heavy Jacket

Page 84

✔ Review: The Movies

1. Have students name six types of films and give examples from current films, if possible, or from previous lesson.

2. Lead a discussion on movies from students' native countries, and on students' favorite films, film stars.

Something New: Clothing

1. Explain objectives to class: They will learn about types of clothing and about the four seasons of the year.

2. Tell the class you are looking in Tomas and Sara's closet.

3. Hold up V49 and say "It's a short dress." Ask "What is it?" Answer "It's a short dress," and have students repeat.

4. Follow the same procedure using V50–V56.

5. Briefly review all 8 items.

6. Draw a "closet" on the board. Explain that this is Tomas and Sara's closet. Have class decide which side of the closet belongs to which person, then put the items of clothing (or have students put them) on the appropriate sides of the closet. (Use tape or the chalk rail to put clothing "in the closet.")

Page 85

☛ Practice: "What's in the closet?"

1. Take each visual from the chalk rail and ask, "What's in the closet?" Put items back, and have class, groups, individuals ask and answer the questions. Also ask yes/no questions, using "Is there…" and "Are there…"

2. Have students open their books and read what they have been practicing orally on the first and second pages of the lesson, as a class, in groups, and in pairs.

Page 86

Something New: Seasons

1. Establish context for talking about seasons by discussing types of clothing worn for warm, hot, cool, and cold weather.

2. Talk about temperatures for the various months of the year.

3. Review the months of the year by having class tell you the months as you write them on the board.

4. Then list the months by season. Name each season. Have class identify the seasons, repeat, and name them.

5. Use adjectives to describe each season. Have class identify, repeat, then describe each season.

☛ Practice: "Are the winter months cold?"

1. Use the months listed on the board to ask and answer questions about the seasons:

   e.g.,   Are the summer months hot?
           Are the winter months cold?
           What's the hot season?
           Is it cold in spring?

2. Have class open their books to the Practice and read what they have been practicing orally.

Let's Talk: You Need a Heavy Jacket*

1. Show the visual to establish the context of the conversation: Sara is trying to persuade her husband to buy some new clothes.

2. Model the dialogue as students listen, indicating the speakers by pointing to the visual or other means.

3. Model the dialogue again.

4. Model the dialogue and have class repeat.

5. Take one role and have class take other role; then change roles.

6. Divide class in half and have them take the two roles; then have them switch roles.

7. Have volunteers say the dialogue for the class.

 8. Have class open books and practice the dialogue in pairs.

*Cassette users can have students listen to the dialogue first with books closed.

Page 87

☞ Practice: "What do you need?"

 1. Use the visuals as cues to practice the verbs *want*, *need*, *have*. Have class practice asking as well as answering yes–no and wh– questions, in third person as well as first and second. Differentiate especially between need and want.

 2. Have class open their books to read what they have been practicing orally, as a class, in groups, and in pairs.

Page 88

■ Interaction: Talk about the Weather

1. Use yourself as an example and tell about your favorite season and the weather you like.

     e.g., T: Fall is my favorite time of the year.
                  I like cool weather.

2. Have half of the class ask and the other half answer questions about you.

     Gr. 1:   What season does T like?
     Gr. 2:   He/She likes fall. etc.

3. Have class ask one student the questions.

     C1:   *(Name)*, do you like cold weather or hot weather? etc.

 4. Have small groups of students ask each other questions about seasons and have a few groups report back to the class.

5. Follow the same procedure to get information about clothing students need for summer, etc.

📼 Reading: At the Department Store*

1. Have class look at visual accompanying the Reading. Explain the meaning of "sale."

2. Have class then read selection independently.

3. Ask oral comprehension questions.

4. Have volunteers practice the dialogue.

*Cassette users can have students listen to the Reading first with books closed.

Page 89 ### *Discussion*

Go over the Discussion questions. Have students answer the questions in groups and report back to the class.

✍ Writing

1. Have class do Writing independently.

2. Correct by checking individual papers, or having students write their answers on the board or on an overhead transparency.

✍✍ More Writing

1. Go over the difference between *want* and *need*. Talk about yourself— expensive items you'd like, sensible items you really need.

2. Instruct students to make two shopping lists for clothing.

3. Discuss as a class.

Lesson 34 Activity Pages

Page 90 ### A. Write about Greta's closet.
Students can do this work independently. They need to fill in the blanks using the vocabulary words in the box.

Page 91 ### B. Write the questions or answers.
Students can also do this independently.

She's Wearing a White Dress

Communication Objectives:

Talk about actions in progress
Identify colors
Describe people by their clothing and actions

New Structures:

Present progressive

Visuals:

V58   standing teacher, 3 students (listening, reading, writing)
V59   Let's Talk: She's Wearing a White Dress

Other instructional aids:

Items of various colors taught in the lesson
(Students'clothing can also be used.)

Page 92

✔ Review: The Seasons and Clothing

1. Ask volunteers to put the seasons up on the board, others to write the months below the seasons. Go over the months and seasons.

2. Review terms hot, warm, cool, cold. Ask students to describe the seasons in their countries. Have volunteers write these descriptions on the board (below each season).

Something New: What Am I Doing Now?

1. Explain the objective of lesson: Students will learn about something happening "now."

2. Make name cards for Mrs. Baker, May, Tony, and Sara. Bring three chairs up to the front of the room. Explain that this is a classroom and that May, Tony, and Sara are some of the students. Have students tell you who Mrs. Baker is (the teacher). Hold the name card and act out the roles of the teacher and each student in turn, modeling what each is doing:

> T: I'm standing and talking, etc.
> I'm listening (cup your hand around your ear). etc.

3. Have class go through Listen and Identify (physically responding), Listen and Repeat, and Listen and Answer phases, as a class, in groups, and individually.

☛ Practice: "She's listening"

1. Use the visual to cue practice about May, Tony, etc.

 2. Have class open their books to the Practice to read what they have been practicing orally, as a class, in groups, and in pairs.

3. Ask both "wh" questions and "Is/Are" questions.

☛ Practice Activity: What are they doing?

1. Give a book to a student, ask what he/she is doing.

> T to S1: What are you doing?
> S1: I'm reading.
> T to C1: What is S1 doing?
> C1: He/She's reading.

2. Give a notebook and pen to another student and follow the same procedure as above.

3. Have volunteers come to the front of the class. Have them stand, sit, listen, read, write, talk (use two students for "talking"). Have class ask students what they are doing, have each respond. Have half of class ask the other half about the student volunteers. [Note: The two students who are talking should answer, "We're talking."]

  Let's Talk: She's Wearing a White Dress*

1. Show the visual to establish the context of the conversation. Ask students who the people in the visual are, where they are, and what the two adults (talking) are doing.

2. Model the dialogue as students listen, indicating the speakers by pointing to the visuals or other means. Explain "describe." Give examples. Explain use of verb "wear" for clothing.

3. Model the dialogue again.

4. Model the dialogue and have class repeat.

5. Take one role and have class take other role; then change roles.

6. Divide class in half and have them take the two roles; then have them switch roles.

7. Have volunteers say the dialogue for the class.

 8. Have class open books and practice the dialogue in pairs.

*Cassette users can have students listen to the dialogue first with books closed.

☛ **Practice: "She's wearing a black sweater"**

1. Pick out a student in class who is wearing a black sweater (or something black) and model: "She/He's wearing a black _____." Next model the question, "What's she wearing?" and have students answer.

2. Have volunteers say the dialogue for the class.

 3. Have class open books and practice the dialogue in pairs.

Page 95 ## Something New: Colors

1. Explain the objective of the lesson: Students will be able to describe people by their clothing and actions.

2. Introduce colors by pointing to clothing students are wearing in the colors listed on the chart. Say each color and have students repeat.

3. Have students identify students wearing various colors.

> T: Who's wearing something red? etc.

4. Have students listen and answer.

> T: What color is Mari wearing?
> C1: She's wearing green.
> T: What's Haidi wearing?
> C1: She's wearing an orange dress.

☛ **Practice Activity: What are they wearing?**

1. Make a transparency of the activity or copy it onto the board.

2. Explain the Practice Activity, using what you are wearing as an example:

> T: I'm wearing a white shirt.
> Fill in my name.
> Draw a line from my name to the color white.
> Draw a line from white to shirt.
> Class, what am I wearing? etc.

2. As students do activity independently, circulate and help those who need more guidance.

Page 96 ## Reading: At the Shopping Mall*

1. Introduce the topic by talking about a well–known mall in your geographical area. Ask class if they like to go shopping there. Take a poll of the mall stores they patronize. Ask if they go to the mall just to look at things but not buy anything.

2. Establish the ages of the characters in the selection. Have class read the story independently.

3. Ask Discussion questions as a comprehension check, and then have students read the passage again.

4. Ask volunteers to read the passage.

*Cassette users can have students listen to the Reading first with books closed.

Page 97   ✍ **Writing**

1. Go over the directions.

2. Have class do the Writing independently; correct as a class.

Lesson 35 Activity Pages

Page 98   **A. Listen and circle the correct picture.***
Explain that students will be listening to dialogues between two people. Say dialogues twice, then go over each item.

Script:
Listen. Circle the correct picture.

1.   May: Do you see Molly? She's wearing a white sweater.
      Sally: What color sweater?
      May: White.

2.   Tom: Do you see Charles? He's wearing a heavy jacket.
      Sam: A heavy jacket?
      Tom: Yes, that's right.

3. Henry: Do you see Mr. Sato? He's wearing a wide black and white tie.
      Jim: I'm sorry. Wide, or white?
    Henry: Wide. A wide, black and white tie.

4.   Alice: Do you see Mabel? She's writing a letter.
      June: Oh, that's Mabel? She's wearing glasses.

*Cassette users can have students listen to the script on tape.

B. Draw a picture of yourself today. Write about what you're wearing.

Make sure students understand that they need to draw pictures and then write descriptions.

 Have students circulate to show and discuss their pictures with others.

C. Match the question with the answer.

Have students work independently. They can check their work with a partner or with the whole class.

D. Look at the picture with your group and write a conversation. Choose people to act out the conversation for the class.

 1. Form groups of 3–4 students. Explain that they will write a dialogue. Lead a discussion on what might be happening in the picture.

2. Have groups choose names for the people in the dialogue and write down the conversation.

3. Have the groups perform their conversation for the class.

He's Watching TV

Communication Objectives:
  Talk about household activities
  Check on children's activities

New Structures:
  None

Visuals:

  V60   Maria is cleaning the house.
  V61   Jim is mowing the lawn.
  V62   Luisa and Cecilia are doing the dishes.
  V63   Salsa is running around.
  V64   Let's Talk: He's Watching TV

Page 102

✔ Review: Colors and Actions

1. Have students name the colors of the rainbow.

2. Have students identify classmates who are wearing these colors. They should also identify the clothing.

3. Ask class members to tell what they are doing right now.

Something New: Saturday Activities

1. Explain the objectives of the lesson: Students will talk about household and children's activities.

2. Ask class if they are busy on Saturday working around their homes. Elicit chores that they perform.

3. Show V60 and say "Maria is cleaning the house." Repeat "cleaning the house" and have students repeat.

4. Follow the same procedure for Jim, Luisa and Cecilia, and Salsa.

5. Briefly review all 4 visuals and activities.

Page 103

☞ Practice: "He's mowing the lawn"

1. Use the visuals to cue the practice. Give students opportunity to ask as well as answer questions.

2. Have class open their books and read what they have been practicing orally.

Page 104 **Let's Talk:** He's Watching TV*

1. Show the visual to establish the context of the conversation. Tell class who people are and their relationship to each other.

2. Model the dialogue as students listen, indicating the speakers by pointing to the visual or other means.

3. Model the dialogue again.

4. Model the dialogue and have class repeat.

5. Take one role and have class take other role; then change roles.

6. Divide class in half and have them take the two roles; then have them switch roles.

7. Have volunteers say the dialogue for the class.

 8. Have class open books and practice the dialogue in pairs.

*Cassette users can have students listen to the dialogue first with books closed.

☛ Practice: "He's in the living room"

 1. Use the dialogue to cue practice. Ask yes–no, Where, and What——doing questions. Give students opportunity to ask as well as answer questions.

 2. Have students open their books to read what they have been practicing orally.

Page 105 ### ■ Interaction: Household Activities

1. Ask class about household chores people perform, either indoors or out-doors. You may need to cue them by acting out some activities.

 2. Have groups prepare and present lists by acting out the various chores. Have the rest of the class guess what these activities are. [Note: groups may identify their pantomime as indoor or outdoor activities.]

3. Write a few of the activities not already in the book on the board.

4. Have class write lists of household activities individually.

Page 106 📼 **Reading:** Babysitters*

    1. Show the dialogue visual again. Identify Luisa in the visual and review her function, that of being a "babysitter."

    2. Read the story to the class as students follow along in their books. Explain new vocabulary.

    3. Ask oral comprehension questions.

    4. Have class read the story independently.

    *Cassette users can have students listen to the Reading first with books closed.

Discussion

Go over Discussion questions, from comprehension questions about the Reading to take–off questions about students themselves and what they do about babysitting.

Page 107 ✍ **Writing**

    1. Have class look at the pictures in the book. Discuss what the people in the pictures are doing.

    2. Read the first sentence. Have class do the rest of the Writing independently.

    3. Have volunteers write sentences on the board.

Lesson 36 Activity Pages

Page 108 **A. Talk about the picture.**
Lead a class discussion about the situation depicted by illustration.

Page 109 **B. Write questions or answers about the picture on page 108.**

Page 110 **C. Roleplay: The Parents Come Home.**
As students finish writing, they can gather in groups to work on a roleplay. One or two groups can report back by acting out their roleplays.

Unit Twelve Evaluation

Page 111 **I. Listening Comprehension***

    1. Go over the directions for Part I with students.

    2. Read each item of the script two times, at normal conversational speed.

Script:
1. That's a wide tie.

2. He needs a summer jacket.

3. It's on sale.

4. He's wearing a belt.

5. She's watching TV.

6. She's a babysitter.

7. Is this a winter shirt?

8. Is she washing dishes?

*Cassette users can have students listen to the script on the tape.

Page 112 **II. Reading and III. Writing**

    1. Go over the directions for Parts II and III with students.

    2. Have class do these sections independently.

Evaluation Check

    1. Correct evaluation by having student volunteers write their answers on the board or an overhead transparency.

    2. Have class check their answers.

    3. Circulate to make sure students have checked their work accurately.

How's Your New Job?

Communication Objectives:
>Talk about a new job
>Discuss things learned on the job or through adult education
>Describe on–the–job activities

New Structures:
>Infinitive after *learn*

Visuals:
>V65   sewing a dress
>V66   baking bread
>V67   typing a letter
>V68   painting a house
>V69   driving a big truck
>V70   selling watches
>V71   Let's Talk: How's Your New Job?

Page 114

✔ Review: Household Activities

1. Go over the directions with the students.

2. Guide students through the steps listed in the text.

Something New: I'm Learning to Do Many Things

1. Explain lesson objectives: That students are going to discuss things learned on the job or at adult school, and describe on–the–job activities.

2. Show V65 and say "I'm learning to sew." Repeat and have students repeat.

3. Follow the same procedure for V66–V70, modeling and repeating only the first sentence associated with each visual.

4. Show visuals again, this time saying both sentences. Add "now" to the second sentence. Go through the procedures of repeating and responding.

5. Review by asking questions using for example, "What are you learning to do?" and "What are you doing now?"

☛ Practice: "What are you learning to do?"

1. Hand out the visuals to various students and ask yes–no questions. Then ask what the people in the visuals are learning to do and what they are doing now, having students respond. Ask the whole class what these students are learning to do, etc. and have class, groups, and individuals respond.

 2. Have class open their books and read what they have been practicing orally.

  ## Let's Talk: How's Your New Job?*

1. Show the visual to establish the context of the conversation: Cecilia's husband is asking her about her first day at work.

2. Model the dialogue as students listen, indicating the speakers by pointing to the visual or other means. Explain *enjoying*.

3. Model the dialogue again.

4. Model the dialogue and have class repeat.

5. Take one role and have class take other role; then change roles.

6. Divide class in half and have them take the two roles; then have them switch roles.

7. Have volunteers say the dialogue for the class.

 8. Have class open books and practice the dialogue in pairs.

*Cassette users can have students listen to the dialogue first with books closed.

☛ Practice: "It's a lot of fun!"

1. Use visuals to cue practice.

> T: Are you enjoying your new job?
> C1: Yes, I am. It's a lot of fun.
> T: Is he enjoying his new job?
> C1: Yes, he is. etc.
> T: Is she enjoying her new job? etc.

Build up the practice by adding the question "What —— doing?"

 2. Have class read the Practice exercise.

■ Interaction: Are You Enjoying Your (New) Job?

1. Explain and model the roleplay activity, using a student volunteer.

2. Have class, then volunteers, practice some sample dialogues before going into pair practice.

★ Something Extra: Learning for Fun

Ask class if anyone is learning to do something new for fun. Introduce the visuals and present Listening, following the usual steps. Have students repeat each activity.

■ Interaction: I'm Learning Something New

1. Go over directions with class. Explain that what students are learning doesn't need to be a formal activity.

2. Have students work in pairs. Then have pairs report to whole class.

▣ Reading: Lifelong Learning*

1. Introduce the topic of Lifelong Learning by talking about the classes offered at the school students are attending.

2. Have class read the selection.

3. Ask oral comprehension questions.

*Cassette users can have students listen to the Reading first with books closed.

Discussion

1. Guide students to understanding question #1. You may want to ask students if lifelong learning is possible where they came from.

2. Have students continue with the rest of the questions.

✍ Writing

You may want to answer the first two questions as a class. Then have the students do the rest of the Writing activity independently.

☛ Practice Activity: Classes

1. Get brochures from the school for this activity. Use the brochures as a reading activity. Discuss the various classes and classify them as education, job training, or fun classes.

2. Have students choose classes that they would like to attend and discuss what qualifications they would need to be in the classes.

Lesson 37 Activity Pages

Page 120 **A. Listen and write the room number under the picture.***
Explain what students are listening for.

Script:
Listen and write the room number under the picture.

There are many classes at A to Z Adult School.
In the main building there are 6 classrooms.
The students are learning to do new things in each class.

In Room 101 they are learning to play the guitar.
In Room 102 they're learning to speak English.
In Room 103 they're learning to bake.
In Room 104 they're learning to drive.
In Room 105 they're learning to type, and in
Room 106 they're learning to sew.

These students like their classes and enjoy learning.

*Cassette users can have students listen to the script on the tape.

Page 121 **B. Look at the pictures on page 120 and write the answers below.**
Students can do this independently.

Lesson 38

I'm Making a Right Turn

Communication Objectives:
Identify actions practiced in a driving lesson
Identify arm signals for driving
Interpret traffic signals

New Structures:
Mean/means to give definitions
Negative imperative *don't*

Visual:
V72   Let's Talk: I'm Making a Right Turn

Page 122

✔ Review: Learning New Activities

1. Have students share any new activities they are learning to do at work.

2. Have students share what they are learning to do that's fun. Share with class any new thing you are learning to do.

Something New: Learning to Drive

1. Go over objectives of the lesson: Students will learn vocabulary and actions connected with driving. They will also learn rules for pedestrians.

2. Sit on a chair in front of the class and tell the class that it's a car. Say: I'm learning to drive. Demonstrate each statement physically as you give each statement. Have students repeat each statement.

3. Call out each statement and have students act out each statement.

4. Act out each statement and have class name it.

5. Cue with statements and model, having class and individuals repeat.

Page 123 **☛ Practice Activity: Driving actions**

> 1. Demonstrate physically and ask: What am I doing? Have class answer: You're——.
>
> 2. Give commands: Start the car. Ask: What are you doing? and have class, groups, individuals respond physically and answer the questions.
>
> 3. Open books and have class read what they have been practicing as a class, in groups, in pairs.

Page 124 **Let's Talk:** I'm Making a Right Turn*

> 1. Show the visual to establish the context of the conversation: A student driver with a driving instructor.
>
> 2. Model the dialogue as students listen, indicating the speakers by pointing to the visual or other means.
>
> 3. Model the dialogue again.
>
> 4. Model the dialogue and have class repeat.
>
> 5. Take one role and have class take other role; then change roles.
>
> 6. Divide class in half and have them take the two roles; then have them switch roles.
>
> 7. Have volunteers say the dialogue for the class.
>
> 8. Have class open books and practice the dialogue in pairs.
>
> *Cassette users can have students listen to the dialogue first with books closed.

☛ Practice: "What are you doing?"

> Ask students to perform physical activities as cues for the Practice. Have class practice asking and answering questions.

Page 125 **Something New:** Rules for Drivers and Pedestrians

> 1. Draw on the board or on a sheet of paper a rectangle with three circles, one under the other, to represent a traffic signal. Identify it and have class tell you what colors are at the top, in the middle, and at the bottom (red, yellow, green). If you have colored markers or colored chalk, you can color the circles.

2. Elicit from class what each color means. Have them repeat: A red light means, etc.

3. Explain "pedestrian." Draw Walk (figure) and Don't Walk (hand) signals. Have class read the signs. Discuss what pedestrians need to do for safety: cross with green light or with Walk sign, and be alert for cars making left turns.

Page 126

■ Interaction: Traffic Signals

1. Go over the examples and practice the question *What does...mean?*

2. Have students work in pairs.

🔲 Reading: Pedestrians*

Have class read the selection. Discuss the vocabulary. You may need to reproduce an intersection on the board, with crosswalks delineated.

*Cassette users can have students listen to the Reading first with books closed.

Discussion

1. Go over questions.

2. Lead class in discussion. You may want to talk about how laws are different in different cities and in different countries after students have answered the questions in the text.

Page 127

✍ Writing

Go over the first two questions as a class. Have class do the rest of Writing exercise independently. Correct exercise.

Delta's Apple Pie, Teacher's Guide 1B

Page 128　　**A. Match the picture to the sentence.**

This can be an independent activity. Follow up with correcting and discussion of diagram.

B. Put the sentences in order. Then say the sentences and give your partner a driving lesson.

Students can do this activity independently and then work with a partner to check their work.

Page 129　　**C. What does this mean? Complete the sentences.**

Students can do this independently. Check as a whole class.

Page 130　　**D. Talk about the picture.**

Ask questions and discuss answers about pictures to elicit discussion.

Page 131　　**E. Read the conversation.**

Read as a class then go into pair practice.

F. Match the questions to the answers.

This is an independent activity.

I'm Studying the Driving Rules

Communication Objectives:
Identify procedure for getting a driver's license
Interpret road signs

New Structures:
Infinitive after *want, need*

Visuals:
V73   driver's license
V74   I need to learn the traffic signs.
V75   I need to learn to drive.
V76   I need to take a test.
V77   Let's Talk: I'm Studying the Driving Rules
V78   Something Extra: More Road Signs

Page 132

✔ Review: Following Directions

1. Review procedures for starting a car and driving.

2. Have half of class be the driving instructor and the other half the driving student, giving and acting out driving a car. Have instructor ask, "What are you doing?" with student answering the question.

Something New: I Want a Driver's License

1. Explain lesson objectives: Class will learn procedures for getting a license and interpret road signs.

2. Show the visual of driver's license, or show your own driver's license. Explain what it is. Have students repeat "driver's license." Model the sentences: I want a driver's license. What do I need to do? Then say, "I need to learn the traffic signs." Have students repeat.

3. Show traffic signs and model. Have students repeat.

4. Show visual and say: "I need to learn to drive." Have students repeat.

5. Show visual and say: "I need to take a test." Have students repeat.

6. Review procedures for getting a license again. Ask class what they need to do to get a driver's license. Have them respond that they need to learn the traffic signs, learn to drive, and take a test.

7. Go over the traffic signs, and have students identify, repeat, and answer what the signs are.

Page 133 ☞ **Practice: "What does she need to do?"**

1. Use a female student as an example.

> T: Lily wants to learn to drive.
>   She needs to learn the traffic signs.
>   She needs to practice driving.
>   She needs to take a driving test.

 2. Have class ask and answer questions about the student, as a class, in groups, and individually.

 Let's Talk: I'm Studying the Driving Rules*

Page 134 & 135 1. Show the visual to establish the context of the conversation: A woman is studying a driver's manual.

2. Model the dialogue as students listen, indicating the speakers by pointing to the visual or other means.

3. Model the dialogue again.

4. Model the dialogue and have class take other role; then change roles.

5. Take one role and have class take other role; then change roles.

6. Divide class in half and have them take the two roles; then have them switch roles.

7. Have volunteers say the dialogue for the class.

 8. Have class open books and practice the dialogue and the following Practice: "She's studying the driving rules" in pairs.

*Cassette users can have students listen to the dialogue first with books closed.

★ **Something Extra:** More Road Signs

Show and model visuals of other road signs, following Listening procedures of identifying, repeating, and answering.

☛ **Practice: "There's a school sign"**

Give class the opportunity to ask as well as answer questions in the Practice.

■ **Interaction:** A Driving Test

1. Review hand signals for left and right turns, stop. Also review mechanical signals (up for right turn, down for left turn, brake for stop). Have students work in pairs and take turns making sure that their partners give the correct signals.

2. Have students work in pairs to give and follow the commands to draw various traffic signs.

📼 **Reading:** Driver Education*

1. Have class make guesses about who and what the Reading is about. Write their guesses on the board. Explain new vocabulary.

2. Have them read the selection. After they finish reading, see if their predictions were correct.

*Cassette users can have students listen to the Reading first with books closed.

Discussion

Go over Discussion questions.

✍ **Writing**

Have class do Writing exercise independently and correct exercise as a class.

Lesson 39 Activity Pages

A. Ask and answer questions about the people.
Have pairs take turns asking and answering questions.

B. Look at the information in A and write the answers.
Go over directions. Have students work independently.

C. Look for someone who...

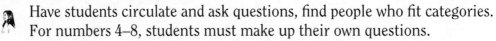 Have students circulate and ask questions, find people who fit categories. For numbers 4–8, students must make up their own questions.

D. Now write three sentences about the students you talked to.
Go over directions. Have students work independently.

Unit Thirteen Evaluation

Page 141 🔲 *I. Listening Comprehension**

    1. Go over the directions for Part I with students.

    2. Read each item of the script two times, at normal conversational speed.

Script:
    1. Don't turn right.

    2. Slow down.

    3. It's okay to cross the street.

    4. I'm steering the car.

    5. Are you learning to drive?

    6. She's learning to type.

    *Cassette users can have students listen to the script on the tape.

Page 142 *II. Reading and III. Writing*

    1. Go over the directions for Parts II and III with students.

    2. Have class do these sections independently.

Evaluation Check
    1. Correct evaluation by having student volunteers write their answers on the board or an overhead transparency.

    2. Have class check their answers.

    3. Circulate to make sure students have checked their work accurately.

I Take the Bus to Work Every Day

Communication Objectives:
> Talk about daily and weekly activities

New Structures:
> Simple present for habitual actions
> Adverbs with *every*
> Questions with *do*

Visuals:

V79	I'm getting up.
V80	I'm eating breakfast.
V81	I'm leaving the house.
V82	I'm walking.
V83	I'm taking the bus.
V84	I'm working.
V85	Let's Talk: I Take the Bus to Work Every Day.
V86	Daily Activities
V87	eat in a restaurant
V88	visit my family
V89	go to the movies

Page 144

✔ Review: Information for Drivers

1. Elicit information from class on what a person needs to do to get a driver's license.

2. Have a student volunteer put the list on the board.

3. Have same or different student sequence list.

4. Ask another volunteer to draw the traffic signs on the board.

5. Have students ask and answer what the signs mean in a chain drill.

Page 145

Something New: I Work Every Day

1. Explain lesson objectives to students: They will talk about daily and weekly activities.

2. Ask students "What are you doing now?" Show V79 and say "I'm getting up." Have students repeat.

3. Follow the same procedure for V80–V84.

4. Show V79 again. Say "I'm getting up. I get up at 6:00 every day." Repeat "I get up at 6:00 every day" and have students repeat.

5. Follow the same procedure for the second statement accompanying V80–V84.

6. Review all 6 visuals again, contrasting between NOW activites and EVERY DAY activities.

7. Hold up visuals at random and have class/group/individuals call out the activity.

Page 146 ☛ **Practice: "She's getting up"**

1. Practice "What's she doing?"

2. Contrast what she's doing now versus what she does every day.

 3. Have class open their books and practice the exercise.

 Let's Talk: I Take the Bus to Work Every Day*

1. Show the visual to establish the context of the conversation: Jae and Tomas are standing at the bus stop.

2. Model the dialogue as students listen, indicating the speakers by pointing to the visual or other means.

3. Model the dialogue again.

4. Model the dialogue and have class repeat.

5. Take one role and have class take other role; then change roles.

6. Divide class in half and have them take the two roles; then have them switch roles.

7. Have volunteers say the dialogue for the class.

 8. Have class open books and practice the dialogue in pairs.

*Cassette users can have students listen to the dialogue first with books closed.

Page 147 ☛ **Practice Activity: What do you do every day?**

1. Have several students take turns asking their classmates, "What do you do every day?"

2. Encourage the students to name different activities.

★ Something Extra: Regular Activities

1. Show V86–V89 and name the activities, using gestures where helpful.

2. Hold up a visual, call out an action, and have students point to the correct activity.

3. Model the captions and have the students repeat.

4. Point to an action and have class/groups/individuals identify.

Page 148

☛ Practice Activity: Daily activities, weekend activities

1. Model asking a student what he does every day and every weekend.

2. Demonstrate, on an overhead transparency or on the chalkboard, how to fill in the grid with the student's name and activities.

 3. Instruct students to interview a different person for each space. Be sure they use the "s" for a 3rd person singular verb.

4. Circulate around the room to help students who need it.

☛ Practice Activity: What are you doing?

1. Have a student stand and perform one of the "regular" activities.

2. Have other students ask:

      S1:   What are you doing?
      S2:   Do you _____ every day/every weekend?

3. The first student will respond.

Page 149

Reading: Every Day Is the Same*

1. Have students look at the illustrations for the story and establish the context.

2. Read the story to the class as students follow along in their books. Ask oral comprehension questions.

3. Have students read the story independently.

4. Have volunteers read the story aloud.

*Cassette users can have students listen to the Reading first with books closed.

Discussion

    1. Go over questions with class.

    2. Lead class discussion.

Page 150 ✍ **Writing**

    Have students refer to the Reading passage to fill in the blanks.

Page 151 ★ **Something Extra:** Your Own Writing

    Have students write about their daily activities, using the actions listed.

Lesson 40 Activity Pages

Page 152 **A. Listen to the sentence and check Now or Every...***

Explain that students must listen to the different situations and decide if the action is something happening now or something that happens every day or every week.

Script

    1. Look at John and Jerry. They're at a party. They're talking and smiling. That's a good party!

    2. Peter works at a garage. He's an auto mechanic. He fixes cars for people. He always does a good job.

    3. Myra works in a restaurant. She cooks lunch and dinner there. She works six days a week. She works hard!

    4. We are sitting in class. Maria is writing, David is reading, and Marta and Sara are practicing their English.

    5. In the morning I wash my face, brush my teeth, and put on my clothes. Sometimes I wash my hair in the morning, too.

    6. Every Saturday I have a day off. I clean my house, wash my clothes, and then I go to a movie. I like my Saturdays!

*Cassette users can have students listen to the script on tape.

Page 153 **B. Group Grid**

    1. Go over directions.

    2. Form groups.

    3. Do one as an example.

Unit Fourteen | Lesson 41

Where Do You Work?

Communication Objectives:
> Talk about places people work
> Talk about hours, days, days off
> Fill out a time card

New Structures:
> Questions with *does*

Visuals:

V90	I work at a video store.
V91	He works at the post office.
V92	They work for a moving company.
V58	They don't work. They're students.
V93	We don't work. We're retired.
V94	She works at home. She's a homemaker.
V95	Let's Talk: Do You Work Every Day?

Page 154

✔ Review: Regular Activities

1. Form partners.

2. Have partners ask each other the questions and report answers to the class.

Something New: I Work at a Video Store

1. Present lesson objectives: Students will talk about where and when people work, and how to fill out a time card.

2. Ask "Where do these people work?" Show V90 and say "I work at a video store." Have students repeat.

3. Follow the same procedure for V91–V94, changing the subject as the visual requires.

4. Review all six visuals.

5. Hold up a visual and have class/groups/individuals give the correct caption.

74

Delta's Apple Pie, Teacher's Guide 1B

Page 155   ☞ **Practice: "Where does he work?"**

    1. Have a student stand in front of the class and act out a job.

    2. Students will try to identify the job.

    3. Have other students take turns performing.

     4. Have students open their books and practice.

Page 156 **Let's Talk:** Do You Work Every Day?*

    1. Show the visual to establish the context of the conversation: May and Tony are talking about May's job.

    2. Model the dialogue as students listen, indicating the speakers by pointing to the visual or other means. Explain "day off."

    3. Model the dialogue again.

    4. Model the dialogue and have class repeat.

    5. Take one role and have class take other role; then change roles.

    6. Divide class in half and have them take the two roles; then have them switch roles.

    7. Have volunteers say the dialogue for the class.

     8. Have class open books and practice the dialogue in pairs.

    *Cassette users can have students listen to the dialogue first with books closed.

☞ **Practice: "How many days a week does she work?"**

    1. Go over visuals.

    2. Have students open books and read the practice items.

Page 157   ★ **Something Extra:** Time Cards

    1. Draw a time card on the chalkboard, or make a transparency of the card in the text.

    2. Fill in the time card as you explain the entries.

    3. Have students open their books and read the text as a class/groups/ individuals.

4. Have the class break into groups of 3–4 and ask each other the questions listed in the text.

5. Have students fill in the blanks.

Page 158 ☛ **Practice Activity: My time card**

1. Using an overhead transparency, go over points of information on the time card.

2. Have students fill in their time cards with their own information.

Page 159 ■ **Interaction:** What Days Do You Work?

1. Go over questions with class.

2. You can have students do this activity in groups or pairs.

★ **Something Extra:** What Do You Do at Work?

1. Show visuals, using gestures where appropriate and demonstrate the job activities.

2. Show several pictures, call out one of the activities, and have students point to the correct picture.

3. Model the captions and have the students repeat.

4. Hold up the visuals and have class/groups/individuals identify the activities.

Page 160 🔊 **Reading:** My New Job*

1. Show the letter and establish context.

2. Have students read independently. Ask oral comprehension questions.

3. Have the students read the story as a class/groups/individuals.

*Cassette users can have students listen to the Reading first with books closed.

Discussion

1. Go over questions with students.

2. Lead the class discussion.

✍ **Writing**

> Have students fill in the blanks, using the words provided.

✍✍ **More Writing**

> 1. Have students write about their own jobs.
>
> 2. Encourage students to share their writings with the class.

┃Lesson 41 Activity Pages┃

A. Listen and match the job with the name.*

> Script:
> 1. Joe answers phones and types letters.
>   He's a secretary in a big office downtown.
>
> 2. Martha fixes the pipes in Joe's building.
>   She's a plumber for the city.
>
> 3. Teresa takes care of her children and husband. She's a homemaker. It's a difficult job, but she loves it.
>
> 4. Victor goes to work very early. He's a truck driver for a big supermarket chain. He gets up at 3:00 a.m.
>
> 5. Ken wants to be a doctor, but he needs to learn many things. He's a student at a medical school downtown.
>
> 6. Yvonne works at the downtown hospital.
>   She's a doctor there. Her job is difficult, but she's very good at it.
>
> *Cassette users can have students listen to the script on tape.

B. Ask and answer questions about the missing information.
> Check to see that Partner A is using page 162; Partner B, page 163.

C. What do you think?
> Have students write the answers on their own.

D. Talk about the picture below.

Page 164

E. Read the story and complete the sentences.

Students do this activity on their own. It is taken from the picture on page 163. You might want to have the whole class and then individuals read this aloud.

Page 165

F. Write the questions or the answers.

Do #1 orally as an example. Have students fill in the blanks according to the story on page 164.

He Paints Cars at Work

Communication Objectives:
    Talk about job duties
    Talk about regular household tasks
    Pronounce –s on verbs

New Structures:
    Contrast of simple present and present progressive

Visuals:

V96	The alarm is ringing.
V97	Tom's putting on his shirt.
V98	He's getting on the freeway.
V99	He's looking for a parking space.
V100	He's signing in.
V101	He's wearing a safety mask.
V102	Let's Talk: Grandmother's Daily Activities

Page 166

✔ Review: What I Do Every Day

1. In groups of three or four, have students ask each other what they do every morning, at work every day, and every evening.

2. Call class together and ask students to report.

Something New: Workday Activities

1. Explain objectives: Students will talk about job duties and household tasks.

2. Show visuals and explain activities, using gestures as necessary.

3. Read each caption and have students repeat.

4. Explain that what the person is doing now is what he does regularly.

5. Hold up a couple of visuals, name an action, and have students point to the correct picture.

6. Model the sentences and have the class/groups/ individuals identify the actions.

Practice Activity: What time does he get up?

    1. Have students hold up pictures of Tom's activities and ask and answer questions about them. Go over examples in text.

     2. Have class open books and practice pages 166–167.

Let's Talk: Grandmother's Daily Activities*

    1. Show the visual to establish the context of the conversation: Mrs. Green asks Alfredo about his grandmother.

    2. Model the dialogue as students listen, indicating the speakers by pointing to the visuals or other means.

    3. Model the dialogue again.

    4. Model the dialogue and have class repeat.

    5. Take one role and have class take other role; then change roles.

    6. Divide class in half and have them take the two roles; then have them switch roles.

    7. Have volunteers say the dialogue for the class.

     8. Have class open books and practice the dialogue in pairs.

    *Cassette users can have students listen to the dialogue first with books closed.

Discussion

    1. Go over questions with class.

    2. Lead class discussion.

★ **Something Extra: Pronunciation**

    1. Have students look at the illustrations and make sentences about each person's activity.

    2. Note that the pronunciation of the 3rd person singular verbs (as well as plurals of nouns) depends on the final sound of the words.

Final sound of verbs	Pronunciation of 3rd person singular	
voiceless	/–s/	speaks, paints, etc.
voiced	/–z/	cleans, stays, etc.
after s, z, sh, ch, or j sounds	/iz/	fixes, washes, etc.

3. Copy the three columns of the lesson on the board, numbering them #1, #2, and #3.

4. Explain the sounds and model the verbs in each column.

5. Have class/groups/individuals repeat.

6. Pronounce a verb and have students indicate with their fingers to which column the word belongs.

☛ Practice: "How do you say this word?"

Copy the list of words on the board and have students pronounce the words.

Page 170 ## ☛ Practice: "What does she do at work?"

1. Direct students to fill in the blanks.

2. Go over the first one with the class.

3. Volunteers can give their answers, reading from their papers.

4. Another volunteer can write the answers on the chalkboard or on an overhead transparency.

Page 171 ## 📼 Reading: Schoolday Activities*

1. Show the illustration and establish context for the story.

2. Read the story to the class as students follow along in their books. Ask oral comprehension questions.

3. Have students read independently.

4. Have volunteers read the story.

*Cassette users can have students listen to the Reading first with books closed.

Discussion

1. Go over questions with students.

2. Lead the class discussion.

✍ Writing

1. Have students fill in the blanks in the story.

2. Have volunteers read their sentences to the class.

```
╔══════════════════════════════╗
║  Lesson 42 Activity Pages    ║
╚══════════════════════════════╝
```

Page 172 📼 *A. Listen and write yes or no.**

Script:

Maria: I'm Maria. I'm Miguel's grandmother. I'm a homemaker. I like to take care of my garden, but right now I'm resting.

1. Is Maria Miguel's wife?
2. Is Maria at work?
3. Does she like to take care of her garden?
4. Is she taking care of the garden right now?

Felicia: My name's Felicia. I work at school. I'm a teacher's aide. I like my job. I'm at home today because my daughter isn't feeling well.

1. Is Felicia at school?
2. Does she work at school?
3. Is she a teacher?
4. Is she taking care of her daughter today?

George: I am George Suzuki. I fix copiers. It's a great job. Today I'm working downtown. Once a year I go to the copier factory and I learn to fix the new copiers. Excuse me, I have to go back to work.

1. Does George fix copiers?
2. Is he studying at the factory now?
3. Is he working downtown?
4. Does he go the factory every day?

*Cassette users can have students listen to the script on tape.

B. BINGO!!

 Go over the rules with the class.

Page 173

C. Write four sentences using the information from BINGO.

Go over the example and then students can complete the writing on their own.

D. Ask and answer the questions with a partner.

Go over the first picture with students; then have them work with partners.

Unit Fourteen Evaluation

Page 175 **I. Listening Comprehension***

    1. Go over the directions for Part I with students.

    2. Read each item of the script two times, at normal conversational speed.

Script:
1. He gets up at six every day.

2. She works in a garage.

3. What's the final sound? Goes. She goes to school at night.

4. She does a little housework.

5. Do they eat in a restaurant every day?

6. Is she washing clothes now?

*Cassette users can have students listen to the script on the tape.

Page 176 **II. Reading and III. Writing**

    1. Go over the directions for Parts II and III with students.

    2. Have class do these sections independently.

Evaluation Check

    1. Correct evaluation by having student volunteers write their answers on the board or an overhead transparency.

    2. Have class check their answers.

    3. Circulate to make sure students have checked their work accurately.

Lesson 43

It Goes West to the Mall

Communication Objectives:
Ask for and give directions for taking the bus
Use north, south, east and west
Give directions by drawing simple maps

New Structures:
Contrast of *Is he...?/Yes, he is* and
Does she...?/Yes, she does

Visuals:
V103   intersection
V104   Let's Talk: It Goes to the Mall

Other instructional aids:
a bus transfer
paper and pens to draw maps

Page 178

✔ Review: What Do You Do?

1. Have groups of three or four ask each other the questions shown in the example.

2. Bring the class together and have individuals tell the class about the people they talk to as shown in the example.

Something New: North, South, East, and West

1. Tell students objectives of the lesson: They will learn about directions.

2. Draw the directional signs N, S, E, W on board as illustrated in text.

3. Point to the sides of the room and name the directions. Have students repeat. [Note: Because some students may not have learned directions in their native language, you may want to discuss in what direction the sun comes up and sets, and you may also find it helpful to talk about the streets around your school and their directions to help students become familiar with the concept.]

4. Draw on the board the bus lines illustrated in the text. Place the school at the intersection of Vermont and Beverly.

5. Draw buses 6, 14, 22, and 11, and show the direction they are traveling. [Note: You may use the names of the streets to match your actual location.]

6. Tell the class which direction and on which street each bus is going. Have them repeat.

Page 179 ☛ **Practice: "Does bus #6 go to the school?"**

1. Cue with the diagram on the board and lead the class/groups/individuals in Practice exercises.

 2. Have class open their books and read the exercises.

Page 180 **Let's Talk:** It Goes to the Mall*

1. Show the visual to establish the context of the conversation: May and Maria are at school, making weekend plans.

2. Model the dialogue as students listen, indicating the speakers by pointing to the visual or other means. Explain "shall" as a suggestion.

3. Model the dialogue again.

4. Model the dialogue and have class repeat.

5. Take one role and have class take other role; then change roles.

6. Divide class in half and have them take the two roles; then have them switch roles.

7. Have volunteers say the dialogue for the class.

 8. Have class open books and practice the dialogue in pairs.

*Cassette users can have students listen to the dialogue first with books closed.

☛ **Practice: "What bus do I take?"**

 1. Cue with a sketch of a bus on the board and lead the class/groups/individuals in practice with items #1–4.

 2. Have students open their books and read the exercises.

Page 181 ★ **Something Extra:** Transfers

1. Show students a transfer or draw one on the board if you don't have one. Elicit that it's a bus transfer. Have students repeat "Transfer."

2. Ask class when you need a transfer. Ask if it costs extra.

☛ Practice: "Transfer to the #45 bus"

 1. Lead class/groups/individuals in practice.

 2. Have students open their books and read the exercises.

Page 182 ### ☛ Practice Activity: A map of the school

1. Tell students that they are going to have a contest to see who can draw the best map. Tell them how long they have to complete the project.

2. Divide class into groups. Select a judge from each group.

3. Have students draw their maps, and judges select the winners.

4. Have winners reproduce their maps on the board or on an overhead transparency.

5. Discuss why the winning maps are good. Award prizes if you wish.

★ Something Extra: Go/Go to/Go to the

 1. Copy on the board the chart for the use of "go/go to/go to the."

2. Model the sentences using these phrases and have class/groups/individuals repeat.

3. Have students ask and answer the drill questions.

 4. Have students open their books and fill in the blanks with "go/go to/go to the."

5. Circulate to check student work, or have students read and/or write their answers on the board for the whole class to check their work.

Page 183 ### 📼 Reading: Does This Bus Go Downtown?*

1. Use the visual accompanying Reading to establish context and for pre–reading predictions.

2. Have class read conversation by themselves.

3. Ask comprehension questions and have students read the conversation again.

4. Have pairs read the conversation to each other and reverse parts.

*Cassette users can have students listen to the Reading first with books closed.

Discussion

    1. Go over discussion questions.

    2. Lead discussion.

✍ Writing

    1. Direct students to look at page 179 in the text.

    2. Have students fill in the blanks independently.

    3. Circulate to check students' work and check as a class orally or by writing answers on the overhead or chalkboard.

Lesson 43 Activity Pages

Page 184 📼 ***A. Listen and mark the direction with an arrow.****

Script:

    1. Go to the intersection of Beverly and Vermont. Go north on Vermont.

    2. Go to the intersection of Beverly and Vermont. Go West on Beverly.

    3. Go to the intersection of Beverly and Vermont. Go south on Vermont.

    4. Go to the intersection of Beverly and Vermont. Go east on Beverly.

    5. Go to the intersection of Vermont and Melrose. Go south on Vermont and turn left on Beverly.

    6. Go to the intersection of Beverly and Ohio. Go west on Beverly and turn right on Vermont.

*Cassette users can have students listen to the script on tape.

Page 185   **B. Read the bus routes and look at the map.**

1. Go over the map with the students.

2. Make sure they understand the directions.

3. Clarify any vocabulary or direction questions.

4. Have students complete the activity on their own.

Page 186   **C. Just for fun: Create a bus route.**

Have students do this activity in groups or on their own.

How Do You Go to Work?

Communication Objectives:
Talk about transportation
Talk about where people live
Use abbreviations for *street*, *avenue*, etc.

New Structures:
Questions with *how*

Visuals:
V105   She takes the bus to work./He carpools.
V106   He drives to work.
V107   They take the subway to work./They walk to work.
V108   Let's Talk: I Come by Bus

Page 188

✔ Review: Does This Bus Go to the Market?

1. Draw a diagram as described in the text, naming the streets after actual streets in your city.

2. Lead the students into asking each other questions about the bus lines.

Something New: She Takes the Bus to Work

1. Tell students objectives of the lesson: They will learn to talk about transportation.

2. Show visuals and describe the different methods of transportation.

3. Model the sentences and have the class/groups/individuals repeat.

4. Ask several students, then have them ask each other
    S1: How do you go to work?
          How do you come to school?

5. Contrast the meanings of "go" and "come."

Page 189

☛ Practice Activity: How do you come to school?

1. Cue with sketches on the board and lead the class/groups/individuals in practice.

2. Have students open their books and read the Practice.

3. Go around the room and have students tell the class how they come to school.

Let's Talk: I Come by Bus*

 1. Show the visual to establish the context of the conversation: Two people are going into work at the same time.

2. Model the dialogue as students listen, indicating the speakers by pointing to the visual or other means.

3. Model the dialogue again.

4. Model the dialogue and have class repeat.

5. Take one role and have class take other role; then change roles.

6. Divide class in half and have them take the two roles; then have them switch roles.

7. Have volunteers say the dialogue for the class.

 8. Have class open books and practice the dialogue in pairs.

*Cassette users can have students listen to the dialogue first with books closed.

Page 190 ## ☛ Practice: "I live on Madison near 9th"

 1. Draw a map on the board showing where you live in relation to a landmark or a well–known street. Explain that you live on _____ Street near _____ .

2. Do this same procedure with a student, asking where he/she lives.

3. Explain the meaning of block, and illustrate on board.

4. Tell how you get to work. Ask a volunteer to tell how he/she gets to work.

 5. Open books and have students read the Practice.

☛ Practice: "How far do you live from school?"

1. Using the same map from the above Practice, explain the word mile. Explain "How far" is the way we ask about distance between 2 points.

2. Have students open their books and read the Practice.

☛ Practice Activity: How far?

1. Have students work in groups asking and answering questions.

2. Have students report back to class.

★ Something Extra: Names of Streets

1. Write *street*, *avenue* and *boulevard* on the board.

2. Show the abbreviations for each.

3. Have students try to think of a local street, avenue and boulevard name. Write them on the board.

4. Have students open their books and read this section.

5. See if students can come up with other street names such as lane, alley, etc. Have them write them in the blanks. Provide the abbreviations if students don't know them.

☛ Practice Activity: Take a poll

Ask how many students live on streets, avenues, boulevards, etc. Discuss any others that come up, such as road, place, etc. Finally, take a poll and count how many students live on each.

📼 Reading: Getting Around*

1. Show class the picture in the text and establish context for the story.

2. Read the story to the class as students follow along in their books. Ask oral comprehension questions.

3. Have students read independently.

*Cassette users can have students listen to the Reading first with books closed.

Discussion

1. Go over questions.

2. Lead class discussion.

✍ Writing

1. Have class do Writing independently.

2. Correct as a class.

Lesson 44 Activity Pages

Page 194 **A. Listen and match the people to the way they get around.***
  1. Go over the directions.
  2. Read the script or play the tape.

      Script:
  1. Mike lives in a big city. There are elevated trains, subways, and buses in his city. He takes the subway to work.

  2. Dinh lives in a small town. He lives about one mile from work and from school, so he rides a bicycle.

  3. Jayme lives very far from work. There's no bus or subway near her house. She needs to drive a car.

  4. Sadae likes to take the bus. She can take the bus everywhere—to work, to the market, even to visit friends.

  5. Joanne says it's healthy to walk. She lives very close to work, and she walks to work every day.

  6. Greta likes to drive with friends. She works near her friend's office, and they carpool together. They like to carpool.

    *Cassette users can have students listen to the script on the tape.

B. Group Grid: How do you get around?
  1. Go over example with students.

 2. Have them work in groups or walk around the room and ask five people the questions.

Page 195 **C. Look at the box and complete the sentences.**
  1. Students can do this activity on their own.

  2. Have a volunteer read the completed paragraph or write the paragraph on the board or an overhead transparency.

D. Write your answers. Then ask your partner the questions.
  1. Students can do this activity on their own.

  2. Model the activity first to make sure students understand directions.

We Danced All Night

Communication Objectives:
> Talk about past activities
> Make small talk about one's day off

New Structures:
> Simple past (regular verbs)
> Preposition *until*
> Contrast of simple past and simple present

Visuals:
> V109   He cleaned his apartment.
> V110   He washed his clothes at the laundromat.
> V111   He played soccer at the park.
> V112   He visited his girlfriend.
> V113   Let's Talk: We Danced All Night

Page 196

✔ Review: How Do You Come to School?

1. Initiate several chain drills: "How do you come to school?"

2. Have several students take a poll of the class, tallying and recording answers on board:

walks _____   drives _____   comes by bus _____

carpools_____   gets a ride _____

Something New: Mark's Day Off

1. Tell students objectives of the lesson: They will talk about past activities and a day off.

2. Introduce Mark and talk about what he usually does on his day off. Show visuals #109–112 and have students identify the action.

3. Establish the past time, using a calendar or showing the days of the week on the board.

> T: What day is today?
> It's Thursday.
> Today is Thursday. Yesterday was Wednesday.
> Every week, on his day off, Mark cleans his apartment.
> Yesterday he cleaned his apartment.

4. Model the past–time sentences and have class/groups/individuals repeat.

5. Show visuals and have class/groups/individuals describe Mark's activities yesterday.

Page 197 ☛ **Practice: "What does Mark do on his day off?"**

1. Using gestures, model the questions and answers.

2. Write the sentences on the board to illustrate the construction of the past tense.

 3. Have students ask each other the questions.

 Let's Talk: We Danced All Night*

1. Show the visual to establish the context of the conversation. Co–workers are talking in a market.

2. Model the dialogue as students listen, indicating the speakers by pointing to the visual or other means.

3. Model the dialogue again.

4. Model the dialogue and have class repeat.

5. Take one role and have class take other role; then change roles.

6. Divide class in half and have them take the two roles; then have them switch roles.

7. Have volunteers say the dialogue for the class.

 8. Have class open books and practice the dialogue in pairs.

*Cassette users can have students listen to the dialogue first with books closed.

Discussion

       1. Go over questions with class.

       2. Lead the class discussion.

Page 198   ☛ **Practice: "I cleaned house all day"**

       1. Cue with visuals, sketches, or gestures and lead the class/groups/ individuals in the practice.

       2. On #5–6, contrast present with past.

Page 199   ■ **Interaction:** My Day Off

       1. Have students take a sheet of paper and make a chart as explained in the text.

    2. Have them walk around the room and collect information from their classmates.

       3. Bring the class together and have them share their findings.

    📼 **Reading:** A Family Evening*

       1. Show class the picture in the text and establish context for the story. Explain new vocabulary (hemmed).

       2. Have students read independently. Ask oral comprehension questions.

       3. Lead the discussion.

       *Cassette users can have students listen to the Reading first with books closed.

Page 200   ✍ **Writing**

       1. Have students answer #1 and #2.

       2. Assign a short paragraph on what the students did on their day off.

Lesson 45 Activity Pages

Page 201   ***A. What did he do on his day off?***
       1. Go over directions for this "information gap" activity.

       2. Make sure Partner 1 is working from page 201, Partner 2 from page 202.

Page 203   ***B. TIC TAC TOE: Pick a square and answer the question.***
       1. Go over rules for the game.

    2. Form groups of five students and divide them into teams. Remind referees that they can ask present or past tense questions. Inform teams that they must answer in the correct tense.

       3. Circulate as the groups play the game.

Page 205 ### I. Listening Comprehension*

1. Go over the directions for Part I with students.

2. Read each item of the script two times, at normal conversational speed.

Script:
1. He's carpooling.

2. She's getting on the bus.

3. It's going east on King.

4. We're going to the park. We need transfers.

5. Does he play soccer on his day off?

6. Did they come by bus?

*Cassette users can have students listen to the script on the tape.

Page 206 ### II. Reading and III. Writing

1. Go over the directions for Parts II and III with students.

2. Have class do these sections independently.

Evaluation Check

1. Correct evaluation by having student volunteers write their answers on the board or an overhead transparency.

2. Have class check their answers.

3. Circulate to make sure students have checked their work accurately.

I Worked in a Bank

Communication Objectives:
> Describe work performed in the past
> Pronounce *–ed* past

New Structures:
> Contrast of simple past and present progressive

Visuals:
> V114 He worked in a bakery.
> V115 She worked in an office.
> V116 He worked in a garage.
> V117 She worked in a department store.
> V118 He worked on a farm.
> V119 She worked in a factory.
> V120 Let's Talk: I Worked in a Bank

Page 208

✔ Review: My Day Off

1. Review day off activities with class. Ask students to talk about their usual day off activities. Then ask what they did on their last day off.

2. Form groups of 4–6 students to discuss day off activities.

3. Have each group take a poll of these activities and report to the class:

> e.g., Two people went to the movies, etc.

Something New: What Did He Do in His Country?

1. Explain lesson objective: That students will describe work they did in the past.

2. Show visuals. Gesture and describe the actions.

3. Say each caption and have students repeat.

4. Call out each action and have class/groups/individuals act it out.

5. Act out an activity and have class/groups/ individuals identify it.

☛ **Practice: "He worked in a garage"**

    1. Cue with visuals to practice items #1–4 and similar drills. In #3 and #4, contrast "where" and "what."

    2. Have students open their books and read the actions and the practice items.

 Let's Talk: I Worked in a Bank*

    1. Show the visual to establish the context of the conversation: Mario is visiting Alicia at her home. He meets her father.

    2. Model the dialogue as students listen, indicating the speakers by pointing to the visual or other means.

    3. Model the dialogue again.

    4. Model the dialogue and have class repeat.

    5. Take one role and have class take other role; then change roles.

    6. Divide class in half and have them take the two roles; then have them switch roles.

    7. Have volunteers say the dialogue for the class.

    8. Have class open books and practice the dialogue in pairs.

    *Cassette users can have students listen to the dialogue first with books closed.

☛ **Practice: "He's attending computer school"** and **"Yes, she did"**

    1. Cue with visuals, set the pattern, and practice #1–6 as a class/groups/pairs. Contrast past tense with present progressive.

    2. Have class open books and read the exercises.

■ **Interaction:** What Are You Doing Now?

    1. As a class, have students respond to questions about where they're from, what they did in their country, and what they're doing now.

    2. Form groups of 4–5 and have students discuss these questions with each other.

    3. After 5 minutes, reform the groups for further practice.

★ Something Extra: Pronunciation

1. Note that the pronunciation of the past tense of regular verbs depends upon the final sound (not the final letter) of the verb itself.

Final sound of verbs	Pronunciation of the past tense
A. voiceless sounds (f, p, k, s, sh, ch)	t – typed
B. voiced sounds (v, b, g, z, j, l, r, m, n and vowels)	d – sewed
C. verbs ending in t or d	Id – painted Id – needed

2. Copy the three columns of lesson on the board, numbering them A, B, and C.

3. Model the verbs in each column.

4. Have class/groups/individuals repeat.

5. Pronounce a word and have students indicate with their fingers to which column that word belongs.

6. Have class/groups/individuals read the sentences in item #2 in the past tense.

📼 Reading: Graciela Needs a License*

1. Show class the illustration and establish context for the story.

2. Have students read the story independently.

3. Ask oral comprehension questions.

4. Have volunteers read the story aloud.

*Cassette users can have students listen to the Reading first with books closed.

Discussion

1. Go over questions with students.

2. Lead the class discussion.

✍ Writing

Have students write a short paragraph for each of the two topics.

Page 214 **A. Listen and match the name with the occupation.***

Script:
1. Carlos worked in a department store.
   He waited on customers.

2. Sue worked in an office. She typed letters.

3. Yasu worked on a farm. He planted rice.

4. Carla worked in a bakery. She baked cakes.

5. Lionel worked in a garage. He repaired motorcycles.

6. Paula worked in a factory. She sewed dresses.

*Cassette users can have students listen to the script on tape.

B. Answer the questions about the people above.

Page 215 **C. Walk around the room and ask about work experience.**

 1. Demonstrate asking and answering the question, then placing the answer on the grid.

2. If you have made an overhead transparency of the grid or are using the board, have volunteers write the answers on the class grid.

What Can You Do?

Communication Objectives:
Talk about occupations
Discuss skills for various occupations

New Structures:
Modal *can*

Visuals:
V121 He's an auto mechanic.
V122 She's a seamstress.
V123 She's a bus driver.
V124 He's an electrician.
V125 He's a plumber.
V126 She's a hairdresser.
V127 Let's Talk: We Have a Flat Tire

Page 216

Review: What Did You Do in Your Country?

1. Write the following chart on the board:

Name	Where I worked	What I did	What I am doing now
Luis	*on a farm*	*planted corn*	*studying English*

2. Call on students to provide the information, then record on the board.

3. Have students tell about each person.

> S: Luis worked on a farm in his country.
> He planted corn. Now he is studying English.

Something New: People and Their Work

1. Explain lesson objectives: Students will talk about occupations and skills.

2. Show visuals and describe each person.

> T: He's an auto mechanic. He can repair cars.

3. Have students repeat the description.

4. Show the visuals and have class/groups/individuals describe each person.

5. Ask "What can a plumber do?" Elicit answer using *can*. Repeat with other five visuals.

Page 217 ☞ **Practice: "He's an electrician"**
"He can fix pipes"
"What can he do?"

1. Cue with visuals and set the patterns for class/group/individual practice with items #1–6. Explain "occupation."

 2. Have students open their books and read the items.

Page 218 **Let's Talk:** We Have a Flat Tire*

1. Show the visual to establish the context of the conversation: Elsa Soto, Roberto and his friend are getting ready to go home from the park when they discover a flat tire.

2. Model the dialogue as students listen, indicating the speakers by pointing to the visual or other means. Explain new vocabulary.

3. Model the dialogue again.

4. Model the dialogue and have class repeat.

5. Take one role and have class take other role; then change roles.

6. Divide class in half and have them take the two roles; then have them switch roles.

7. Have volunteers say the dialogue for the class.

 8. Have class open books and practice the dialogue in pairs.

*Cassette users can have students listen to the dialogue first with books closed.

☞ **Practice: "Yes, she can"**

 1. Cue with visuals and/or gestures and set the patterns for class/group/pair practice of items #1–4. Introduce "can't" for negative form.

 2. Have students open their books and read the exercises.

★ Something Extra: More People and Their Work

1. Use visuals and gestures to introduce more occupations and their functions.

2. Model the sentences and have students repeat.

3. Model the actions and have students identify them.

☛ Practice Activity: What else can they do?

Elicit from students other functions that people in these occupations can perform and list on the board:

Occupation	What they can do
auto mechanic	repair motors, change tires, etc.

🔲 Reading: The Homemaker*

1. Discuss the role of a homemaker and establish context. Explain "spouse."

2. Have students read the story independently. Ask oral comprehension questions.

3. Read the story as a class/groups/individuals.

*Cassette users can have students listen to the Reading first with books closed.

Discussion

1. Go over questions with students.

2. Lead the class discussion

✍ Writing

Have students rewrite the reading selection in the past tense.

Page 222   **A. Listen and circle the correct picture.***

> **Script:**
> 1. She can drive a bus. She's a bus driver.
>
> 2. He can fix cars. He's a mechanic at Mike's garage.
>
> 3. He can change tires. He worked in a garage in his country.
>
> 4. She can paint beautiful pictures. She's an artist.
>
> 5. She can arrange flowers. She worked for a florist in her country.

> *Cassette users can have students listen to the script on tape.

Page 223   **B. Read and answer the questions. Then ask your partner.**
Go over the directions with class.

Page 224   **C. BINGO!!**
 Go over rules. Remind students they must have a different person sign each box. You might want to have a prize to award winner(s).

Page 225   **D. Talk about the pictures.**
Students can do this activity in groups. Start them off by reading Jack's answer and asking what Ms. Green asked him, etc.

E. Write the questions from the dialogue.
Individuals or groups can write the questions they came up with in D.

F. Act out the interview with your partner.
Ask volunteers to act out the interview, taking the roles of Jack Ho and Ms. Green. Advanced students might want to take the interview even further.

I Can't Take Shorthand

Communication Objectives:
Talk about own talents and skills
Talk about skills for entering the job market

New Structures:
Contrast of *can* and *can't*

Visuals:

V128   I can sing, but I can't dance.
V129   He can read English, but he can't speak it.
V130   He can cook, but he can't bake.
V131   She can type, but she can't take shorthand.
V132   He can stand, but he can't walk.
V133   Let's Talk: I Can't Take Shorthand

Page 226

✔ Review: Occupations

1. Elicit from class the names of the occupations they know.

2. Write the occupations on the board.

3. Elicit what people in these occupations do.

Something New: What I Can't Do

1. Explain lesson objectives: That students will talk about their own skills.

2. Show the first visual and say "I can sing, BUT I can't dance." Have students repeat.

3. Follow the same procudure for the other 4 visuals.

4. Model the sentences and have class/groups/individuals repeat.
   [Note: Contrast the pronunciation of "I can sing/I can't sing" by pronouncing can /kən/ with very weak stress in the affirmative and pronouncing can't /kænt/ with heavier stress in the negative.]

5. Cue with visuals and/or gestures and have class/groups/individuals make sentences with *he/she can/can't*.

6. Ask, "Who can sing?" "Who can't dance?"

6. As students respond, have others comment,

> S: Bill can sing, but he can't dance.
> Bill can sing; Mark can't dance.

Page 227   ☛ **Practice: "Yes, I can" or "No, I can't"**

Have students open books and practice in pairs.

Page 228 **Let's Talk:** I Can't Take Shorthand*

1. Show the visual to establish the context of the conversation: Mona is applying for a job.

2. Model the dialogue as students listen, indicating the speakers by pointing to the visual or other means. Explain "shorthand" and "office clerk."

3. Model the dialogue again.

4. Model the dialogue and have class repeat.

5. Take one role and have class take other role; then change roles.

6. Divide class in half and have them take the two roles; then have them switch roles.

7. Have volunteers say the dialogue for the class.

8. Have class open books and practice the dialogue in pairs.

*Cassette users can have students listen to the dialogue first with books closed.

Page 229   ★ **Something Extra:** Pronunciation

1. Copy the two columns of lesson on the board, numbering the columns.

2. Model the verbs in both columns. Indicate that in the affirmative the stress is on the verb, while in the negative, it's on the modal.

3. Have class/groups/individuals repeat.

5. Pronounce a word and have students indicate with their fingers to which column the word belongs.

6. Have class/groups/individuals read the sentences.

📼 **Reading:** A Musician's Life*

1. Show visual and establish context.

2. Have students read independently. Ask oral comprehension questions.

3. Read the story as a class/groups/individuals.

*Cassette users can have students listen to the Reading first with books closed.

Discussion

1. Go over questions with students.

2. Lead class discussion.

Page 230 ## ✎ **Writing**

1. Assign the Writing exercise

2. Go over #1 with students to orient them to the task.

☛ **Practice Activity**

1. Have students make three lists independently, of things they can/can't/want to do.

 2. Form groups. Have students read and talk about their lists to group members.

Lesson 48 Activity Pages

Page 231 **A. Listen to the people. Circle can or can't.***

Script:
1. Martha can cook. She makes wonderful spaghetti.

2. Jim can't cook, but he likes to eat.

3. Will can't speak Spanish, but he wants to learn.

4. Roger can't repair cars. He never worked as a mechanic.

5. Susan can drive a car. She can even drive a big truck.

6. Jung can type, but he can't use a computer.

*Cassette users can have students listen to the script on tape.

B. Talk about the chart.

Have students do this activity in groups or pairs. Go over the graph with the class. Ask a volunteer to show the class how to question and answer using the graph.

Page 232

C. Use the information from the chart to write sentences.

Help students make the transition from the chart to writing about the information on the chart.

D. Ask three students about what they can do.

Guide students in filling out the chart.

E. Use the information in exercise D to write sentences.

Students should write sentences about their classmates like they did for C. above.

Unit Sixteen Evaluation

Page 233 **I. Listening Comprehension***

   1. Go over the directions for Part I with students.

   2. Read each item of the script two times, at normal conversational speed.

   > **Script:**
   > Listen to the teacher. Circle the letter of the correct answer.
   >
   > 1. She worked in a factory.
   >
   > 2. She can't walk.
   >
   > 3. She's a florist.
   >
   > 4. He can fix cars.
   >
   > 5. Did Ellen watch TV last night?
   >
   > 6. Is she giving a haircut?

   *Cassette users can have students listen to the script on the tape.

Page 234 **II. Reading and III. Writing**

   1. Go over the directions for Parts II and III with students.

   2. Have class do these sections independently.

Evaluation Check

   1. Correct evaluation by having student volunteers write their answers on the board or an overhead transparency.

   2. Have class check their answers.

   3. Circulate to make sure students have checked their work accurately.

Notes

Notes

Delta's Apple Pie, Teacher's Guide 1B